A Model Social Service Program for a County Jail

Social, Educational Research and Development, Inc.

The Praeger Special Studies program—utilizing the most modern and efficient book production techniques and a selective worldwide distribution network—makes available to the academic, government, and business communities significant, timely research in U.S. and international economic, social, and political development.

A Model Social Service Program for a County Jail

Praeger Publishers   New York   Washington   London

PRAEGER SPECIAL STUDIES IN U.S. ECONOMIC AND SOCIAL DEVELOPMENT

PRAEGER PUBLISHERS
111 Fourth Avenue, New York, N.Y. 10003, U.S.A.
5, Cromwell Place, London S.W.7, England

Published in the United States of America in 1972
by Praeger Publishers, Inc.

Library of Congress Catalog Card Number: 70-186200

Printed in the United States of America

The purposes of this study were to determine the need for and design of a broadly based system of social services for a new detention center to replace the old and obsolete jail in Prince George's County, Maryland (adjacent to Washington, D.C.).

The local jail is the arrested person's first point of contact with the correctional system in the United States. It follows at this level that maximum effort should be made to divert the person arrested from further contact with corrections and to assist him to return to society as a productive human being.

Most people who pass through jails are poorly educated, have job difficulties, are drug users and/or alcoholics, or have family or a variety of other problems. Also, when a person lands in jail, he is often at "rock bottom." He may have been unemployed for days or weeks and is probably destitute; he may have been on a drinking spree and not eating or sleeping regularly; he may have been injured in a fight or in an accident; he may be having family problems; and, most certainly, he is in trouble with the law. Thus, jails are in a unique position: They should be able to provide a range of services to needy individuals at their first point of contact with the criminal justice system. This special role of jails and the special problems of many jail inmates were the bases for this study. This volume focuses on needs for a broadly based system of social services in the newly planned jail or detention center.

The corrections situation in Prince George's County is not much different than it is elsewhere in the United States. Most jails are old and out of date. Very few do more than warehouse inmates until they are turned loose or moved to the next step in the system. The general conclusion of the study was that intensive social services should receive a high priority in the newly planned detention center. The basic plan presented here—scaled up or down depending on the jail's population—is appropriate to any jail in the United States.

Some 7,000 persons pass through Prince George's County Jail annually. Most are charged with minor offenses and stay for short periods of time. However, many come back time after time and eventually are involved with serious charges. The overwhelming majority of persons incarcerated in the jail have multiple social and personal problems. They are more likely than most county residents to be unemployed, poorly educated, and have health and other problems. Nevertheless, because of overcrowding and lack of facilities, the present jail provides next to nothing in the way of social services for inmates.

For example, on a typical day, there were more than 75 persons, about 40 percent of the jail's population, who had been in the jail longer than 60 days. Save for television and an occasional visit from a chaplain, these persons, as well as all others in the jail, are denied social services. There are some old books and magazines in the jail, but no program of library services, no counseling, no job assistance, and no educational services: In other words, there is next to nothing to assist these people to rehabilitate themselves, to amuse themselves, and generally to pass the long hours in jail. Not only is this denial brutal, but storing people like this contributes to management difficulties in the jail and, of course, has no corrective impact.

A detention center should contain a network of programs ranging from and including education, training, rehabilitation, counseling, and library services for any interested inmate. Thus, we propose the creation of a social-service center in the new institution. This unit would become the nerve center for programs provided by county and state agencies and volunteer groups.

Any inmate should be able to receive services from this center. Services should be linked to a multilevel program that would range from maximum security, to work and education release in the institution to community-based residential facilities. The amount of services that an inmate receives should depend on the amount of time he spends in the institution.

This study presents a three-step plan. First, there should be immediate plans to improve conditions in the existing jail. Some of these efforts include the present program to provide exercise space and air conditioning. In addition, the population of the jail should be reduced by 20 to 30 persons who would be enrolled in work release and community-based treatment programs. This reduction in the population would make it possible to begin limited social services in the present jail.

The second phase of the program could start in 1975, or sooner, when the new detention center is available. This phase should begin operation of the social-service center and the vast array of services that can be offered in the center. The third phase should start in 1980 and would bring the social-service center to full strength.

Once implemented, the annual cost for this program will be approximately $540,000. This will require only about $150,000 annually in new money from the Sheriff's Department, because most of the funds will come from existing programs at the county and state levels and the transfer of resources from existing expenditures in the Sheriff's Department.

John W. McCollum, President
Social, Educational Research
and Development, Inc.

CONTENTS

PART II: THE PROGRAM

LIST OF TABLES

LIST OF FIGURES

CORRECTIONAL INSTITUTION

SCOPE AND BACKGROUND

This is a study of the potential of a county detention facility
(jail) to provide a wide range of rehabilitation programs for inmates.
Most studies of correctional systems conclude that institutions with
the greatest possibilities but the most poorly developed, are at the
local and county levels. One publication concluded as follows:

> In the vast majority of city and county jails and local
> short-term institutions, no significant progress has been
> made in the past fifty years.
>
> The deeper the offender has to be plunged into the
> correctional process and the longer he has to be held
> under punitive (though humane) restraints, the more
> difficult is the road back to the point of social restoration.
> It is logical, then, to conclude that the correctional pro-
> cess ought to concentrate its greatest efforts at those
> points along the criminal justice continuum where the
> largest numbers of offenders are involved and the hope
> of avoiding social segregation is greatest. . . . On the
> correctional continuum, jails are at the beginning of the
> penal or institutional segment. They are, in fact, the
> reception units for a greater variety and number of
> offenders than will be found in any other segment of the
> correctional process, and it is at this point that the
> greatest opportunity is offered to make sound decisions
> on the offender's next step in the correctional process. [1]

Local jails and institutions are different from state institutions; they usually house a smaller number of inmates, most of whom are awaiting court action and are not under sentence. Inmates in local institutions usually spend short periods of time in the jail, but they often arrive with a host of personal, social, physical, and emotional problems. In addition, local institutions have a less dramatic impact on the general public and are less known than larger, state institutions. Thus, they are often neglected or shunted off by county and local governments and provided with only the most minimal services and facilities.

The potential for rehabilitation at the jail level is probably greater than for other types of institutions. As the report cited above noted, local institutions or jails are the individual's first contact with the correctional system, and it is in these institutions that the rehabilitative process should start. But the same study pointed out that less than 3 percent of the positions in jails and local institutions were filled by social workers, psychologists, psychiatrists, and academic and vocational teachers. The overwhelming majority of staff positions were custodial and administrative.

What makes this significant is the fact that since the mid-1960s an exciting revolution has been underway in the delivery, function, nature, and quantity of social services available in the United States. Included in these efforts are the poverty program, adult basic education, educational assistance for the disadvantaged, programed instruction, manpower training, and so forth. At the process level, new approaches have been developed in teaching, reaching people with problems, and focusing on social, physical, and personal problems. Yet, by and large, this revolution has bypassed local correctional institutions.

The typical person in a local jail arrives in a state of emotional shock, economically destitute, and at odds with his family. He may be a drug user or a problem drinker; he is apt to have health problems. He may need legal services. More often than not, he has difficulty in adjusting to the prison environment. It is at this point that social services should start—not when he arrives at or leaves the penitentiary.

A basic premise of this study is that the person (and his family as well) newly arrived in a local institution can benefit from a variety of services—welfare, educational testing and guidance, vocational guidance, vocational rehabilitation, mental and physical health, legal and financial. Those who stay relatively long periods of time can benefit from specific programs. Also, those who leave jails, whether for another institution or on release or parole, are in need of these services.

This study presents a model social-service delivery system for the planned detention center in Prince George's County, Upper Marlboro, Maryland. In Prince George's County, the present institution is an old, soon to be abandoned, typical county jail. Plans are underway to replace it with a new facility. The social-service program proposed here is designed to fit the new institution.

OBJECTIVES

The basic objective of this study was to identify and design the most effective social-service system possible for the planned detention center.[2] Specifically, the study had the following objectives:

1. To analyze services now available in the institution.

2. To describe the accomplishments and problems of the system to date.

3. To describe factors that may impede development of the most effective social-service system.

4. To analyze present and possible relationships between the county detention center and the state correctional system.

5. To design and recommend an improved social-service system for the county in terms of goals, functions, operations, procedures, and cost.

6. To relate the state of the art in the provision of social services for disadvantaged youth and adults (especially in prison settings) to programs currently underway in the county system.

7. To explore the possibilities and contributions that might be made by such developments as reality therapy, programed learning, halfway houses, community-based training, a video-based education-training program, work release, education release, industry-sponsored education and training, and other new techniques, methods, and systems.

8. To identify areas of financial support.

9. To specify (when appropriate) physical facilities and equipment needs.

As stated above, our purpose was to design a model social-service system for the planned detention center in Prince George's County. Our aim was to maximize the provision of social services to inmates and to relate the services to the inmates' next move, i. e., the street or another institution.

PROCEDURE

In conducting this study, we employed six basic methods and techniques:

First, from intake files in Prince George's County Jail, a random sample of names was drawn from the files of persons incarcerated in 1968, 1969, and 1970. A total of 589 cases for all years were reviewed. (In each year the sample represented about 2 percent to 3 percent of those processed through the jail; this included 209 cases for 1968, 219 cases for 1969, and 161 cases for in 1970.) Data taken from these cases included names, addresses, sex, charges, previous correctional history, and so forth. These data provided the major statistical material in the study. They are particularly important in providing an over-all picture of the kinds of inmates in the institution and the changes that occurred in the population of the institution over the years 1968-70.

Second, the basic sample described above was used to draw an additional sample of persons to be interviewed in depth. The first step was to draw a sample of 180 names from the basic intake sample. We then attempted to interview these people. As might be expected, in this task we encountered a great deal of difficulty because of false addresses, mobility of people, and so forth. As a result, it was necessary to draw more than 150 additional names from the basic sample to complete the interviews. A total of 105 interviews were collected. These interviews were conducted in homes, the jail, and state institutions. The purpose of these interviews was to gather in-depth data on persons who had been processed through the jail.

A third basic method was depth interviews with persons employed in the county and state. We interviewed county and state officials who had responsibility for and/or awareness of social-service programs in the county. These persons were interviewed in terms of their attitudes and concepts of programs in the jail and attitudes toward jail-based, social-service programs.

A fourth approach involved interviews with staff in the county sheriff's office.

A fifth approach involved visits to other jails in the state to identify programs and services underway elsewhere. Jails in six counties were visited: Anne Arundel, Baltimore, Frederick, Harford, Howard, and Montgomery.

Finally, during this study, we read and reviewed a variety of studies relating to social service programs, especially in correctional settings.

In Chapter 2, we will review the social setting in Prince George's County, especially in terms of correctional trends.

NOTES

1. Correction in the United States: A Survey for the President's Commission on Law Enforcement and Administration of Justice (New York: National Council on Crime and Delinquency, 1966), pp. 137-38.

2. This section is adapted largely from the following publication: Social, Educational Research and Development, Inc., "A Proposal for a Survey and a Plan of Action for the Provision of Extended Social Services in the Montgomery County and Prince George's County Detention Centers" (Silver Spring, Md.: SERD, Inc., December, 1969), p. 4. (Mimeographed)

2

DEMOGRAPHIC SETTING

Prince George's County, Maryland, is a 486-square-mile area. It lies north and east of Washington, D.C. and borders on more of the district than any of the counties in Virginia or Montgomery County, Maryland. As a social phenomenon, Prince George's County is a fascinating complex and contains such diverse elements as the University of Maryland, Bowie State College, and old-line tobacco and truck farms. Some small communities in the county, especially along Highway 301 and the Patuxent River, seem to have been motionless for decades. And, many of the county's black residents descended from freed slaves who settled along the district line at the end of the Civil War. The county contains vast tracts of inexpensive apartments and affluent communities such as Bowie, Montpelier, and Tantallon.

Because the county borders on so much of Washington D.C., it is to be expected that the social problems of the county will be similar to those experienced in the district. The county has grown tremendously in recent years, and there are no signs that this growth will decline or slow down. In 1940, the county's population was nearly 89,500; by 1950, it had more than doubled and was about 194,000; in 1960, it had nearly doubled again and was over 357,000; by 1970, it had almost doubled again and was over 660,000.[1] The county has had the highest rate of growth in the metropolitan area; from 1960 to 1970, the population increased by about 85 percent. Montgomery County increased by about 53 percent, and Washington, D.C. declined by 1 percent.[2] Projections to 1980 place the population of Prince George's County somewhere in the neighborhood of 1 million.[3] Such rapid and unprecedented growth was and is bound to bring problems in housing, racial and ethnic relations, schools, municipal government, and, of course, crime.

Unlike adjoining Montgomery County which has several major population centers (the Rockville, Bethesda-Chevy Chase, and the Silver Spring areas), the population of Prince George's County is less dense: About two thirds of the county is in unincorporated areas. Prince George's County is much less affluent than Montgomery County and, as one might suspect, the crime problems are much different. For example, in 1968, about 49 percent of all families in Prince George's County had incomes in excess of $10,000; in Montgomery County, 65 percent were in that income bracket. At the other end of the scale, 16 percent of the families in Prince George's County had an income of less than $6,000; in Montgomery County, 11 percent were in that category. [4]

CORRECTIONAL FLOW

An individual enters the correctional system upon arrest, and in Prince George's County, of the total arrested, only a small proportion ever reach the jail. In the county, some 20 municipalities have police departments which make arrests or issue summonses. Data were not available on the arrest activity of all these municipalities (the state police, U.S. park police, etc.), but in 1970, the county police arrested about 42,000 persons, including persons arrested for traffic violations. If traffic cases are excluded, about 12,000 persons were arrested. [5]

In the county, persons arrested by the county police are taken to the lockups at Hyattsville, Oxon Hill, Bowie, or Seat Pleasant; there, a justice of the peace sets bond, and the individual either makes bond or is sent to jail.

Figure 1 is a rough approximation of the inmate flow process. This figure is oversimplified because many of the persons arrested come from out of the county. Furthermore, it does not show the real flow process in that persons who serve time in the jail or are transferred to another institution are those who are most apt to have been through the system at various levels in the past. However, the treatment of data in this crude fashion suggests that the point of entry for rehabilitation programs in the correctional system should be at the jail level where about one third of all those arrested stop, however briefly.

FIGURE 1

Estimated Inmate Flow Process in the County
Detention and Correctional System

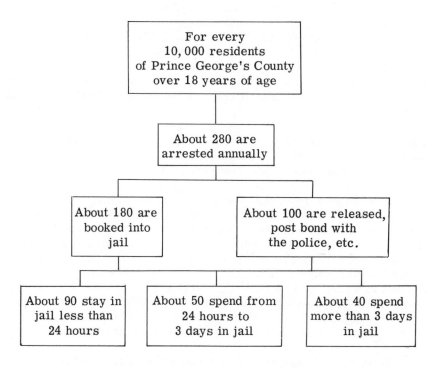

The above figures were computed by using the estimated 1970
population of Prince George's County (660,000) with about 60 percent
of the population 18 years of age and over. In computing the number
of persons arrested, traffic cases were excluded; thus, the 12,000
arrests figure was used. For the number of persons booked into the
jail, the annual population of the jail of about 7,000 was used. The
figures for time spent in jail were computed from data used in Table
14. All figures were rounded off.

THE COUNTY JAIL AND PLANS FOR THE FUTURE

The county jail division is one of five subdivisions within the sheriff's office. This unit operates the main jail in Upper Marlboro and the annex in the County Service Building in Hyattsville. The main jail is located in the complex of county buildings in Upper Marlboro. The facility is old with a rated capacity of about 90 persons. According to a report from the sheriff's office in August, 1969, the highest daily count that year was 240, and the lowest was 137; the average daily population was 165. For 1970, as pointed out later, all of these data are slightly higher, and one can expect the population to continue to grow in the future. How much growth must the system accommodate in the future? This is difficult to ascertain because of many intangible factors, such as the future composition of the population, attitudes toward crime, and so forth. Let us take one indication: The county's population was expected to grow from about 660,000 in 1970 to as high as 1.2 million by 1980.[6] If the jail population increases at the same rate, it should be able to accommodate nearly 300 persons by 1980.

The jail is a traditional institution: It serves the county courts and functions almost completely as a holding operation for persons awaiting trial. A small proportion of persons are under sentence in the jail. In 1971, it was a policy of the courts to sentence a person for more than six months to the state system, rather than to the overcrowded county facility. The present institution provides almost nothing in the way of programs and services. Overcrowding, lack of staff, and inadequate facilities explain the fact that in the old institution it was not possible to offer recreational programs, library services, grouping of inmates by type, education programs, and so forth.

In 1970, a newspaper article about the jail described it as a "lesson in degradation," and as a "human warehouse where [the prisoners] come back into society continuing to live like the subhumans we have forced them to believe they are."[7]

The sheriff began planning for a new facility in 1969. This facility, to be called Prince George's County Detention Center, progressed to the point where a site and an architectural firm had been selected. Some general plans were submitted, but no decisions have been made that might in any way affect the basic ideas of this study.

NOTES

1. U.S. Bureau of the Census, "1970 Census of Population, Maryland, Final Population Counts, Advance Report" (Washington, D.C.: Bureau of the Census, January, 1971), p. 3; U.S. Bureau of the Census, County and City Data Book, 1962 (A Statistical Abstract Supplement; Washington, D.C.: U.S. Government Printing Office, 1962), p. 172.

2. U.S. Bureau of the Census, "1970 Census of Population, Maryland, Advance Report" (Washington, D.C.: Bureau of the Census, January, 1971), p. 3; U.S. Bureau of the Census, "1970 Census of Population, District of Columbia, Advance Report" (Washington, D.C.: Bureau of the Census, December, 1970), p. 1.

3. Doxiadis Urban Systems, Inc., Fiscal and Land Use Analysis of Prince George's County, Volume II (Washington, D.C.: Doxiadis Urban Systems, Inc., June, 1970), p. 5.

4. Doxiadis Urban Systems, Inc., Fiscal Analysis of Montgomery County (Washington, D.C.: Doxiadis Urban Systems, Inc., June, 1970), p. 19.

5. Data from Prince George's County Police Department, Records Section, February, 1971.

6. Doxiadis, Fiscal and Land Use Analysis, loc. cit.

7. "Prince George's Inmate Calls Jail Complete Hell," The Washington Post, July 12, 1970, pp. A1, A10.

3

**INMATE
CHARACTERISTICS
AND COURT ACTIVITY
IN PRINCE GEORGE'S
COUNTY**

This chapter contains data on characteristics of persons processed through the county jail. The data were derived from a variety
of sources: Over 100 interviews were conducted with inmates and
former inmates in the jail, in home communities, and in other institutions. A sample of nearly 600 names going back to 1968 was
drawn from the jail's intake files, and basic personal and social data
for this sample were summarized from these files. Other sources
were used including court records, probation and parole information,
and so forth.

However, there is a basic technical problem about the data
describing characteristics of the inmates. Data collected on inmates
for an annual period describe the kinds of people processed through
the institution and the changes that occur in the inmate population
from year to year. Because of the status of records in the jail, these
data were easiest to collect. Nevertheless, these data do not describe
the inmate population of the jail on a given or typical day. We have
tried to collect some daily population data to sketch out the characteristics of the population on a typical day, but this project was for
a limited period. Hence, we were only able to collect data on several
days.

There is no such person as a typical inmate, but if there were,
we would describe him as follows: He is a white male between 19
and 30 years of age. (However, there are increasingly higher proportions of 18- and 19-year-old males being processed through the
jail.) He is not married. He may be employed; about half are. When
he works, he works in a blue-collar job. He resides in Prince
George's County.

About 9 out of 10 of the persons arrested claimed they had not been previously arrested although about 5 percent reported at least 3 arrests. About half the persons processed through the jail stayed less than 24 hours. However, on a typical day, about 3 out of 10 had been there from 30 to 90 days. Another 3 out of 10 had been incarcerated for more than 90 days.

This suggests that the majority of persons moving through the jail move in and out quickly and stay less than 24 hours, but the jail contains a large residue of long-term inmates. In terms of criminal charges; homicide, robbery, assault, and burglary (generally the hard crimes) are charged against less than 10 percent of the inmates. Other lesser charges, including auto and traffic cases, constitute about 30 percent of the charges against inmates. Charges for narcotics violations showed a slight increase over the years. However, in most cases, alcohol is associated with the arrest.

In terms of release status; over half were able to post bond and obtain their release. Less than 10 percent served time in the jail or in another institution.

PERSONAL CHARACTERISTICS

About 90 percent of those processed through the jail are male, and the proportion has been relatively steady since 1968.

About 50 percent of those processed through the jail were between 19 and 30 years of age. (See Table 1.) The next largest group were those between 31 and 40 years of age and constituted about 16 percent of the total. Youthful offenders (those under 18 years of age) were also a fairly large group: Nearly 20 percent of those incarcerated f rom 1968 to 1970 were 18 years of age or under. When we examine the data in Table 1 for each year, it appears that the proportion of young people is increasing. Also, these data on the pro- portion of young people underrepresent the total number of young people arrested. Most of those under 18 do not go to the jail but are released to their parents or are confined to the Thomas J. S. Waxter Children's Home in Anne Arundel County.

Data in Table 1 were derived from a sample of inmates pro- cessed through the jail from 1968 through 1970. Also, we collected data on a group of inmates in the jail on a so-called typical day in November, 1970. (See Table 2.) These data indicate that younger inmates are more likely to spend more time in the institution than

TABLE 1

Age Groups of a Sample of Persons Processed Through the County Jail, 1968-70

Age Groups	1968 No.	1968 Percent	1969 No.	1969 Percent	1970 No.	1970 Percent	Total No.	Total Percent
16 years and under	15	7.2	16	7.3	23	14.3	54	9.2
17-18 years	21	10.1	20	9.1	21	13.0	62	10.5
19-30 years	92	44.0	106	48.4	80	49.7	278	47.2
31-40 years	41	19.6	39	17.8	14	8.7	94	15.9
41-50 years	31	14.8	27	12.3	9	5.6	67	11.4
51 years and over	9	4.3	11	5.1	14	8.7	34	5.8
Total	209	100.0	219	100.0	161	100.0	589	100.0

TABLE 2

Age Groups of Inmates in the County Jail,
Selected Day, November, 1970

Age Groups	No.	Percent
16 years and under	8	4.1
17-18 years	35	18.1
19-30 years	115	59.6
31-40 years	26	13.5
41-50 years	5	2.6
51 years and over	4	2.1
Total	193	100.0

older inmates. For example, in the institution on the selected day, about 22 percent of the inmates were 18 years of age or under as compared to about 20 percent of the total processed through the jail from 1968 through 1970. However, there is a considerable range; from 17.3 percent in 1968 to 27.3 percent in 1970. Although not shown in either table, about 45 percent of those in the jail on the typical day were in the 19 through 25 age group as opposed to about 35 percent who were processed through the institution from 1968 through 1970. What the higher proportion of young inmates in the institution on a single day probably means is that young people are charged with more serious offenses and/or are unable to make bail, or a combination of the two factors. This is an important point: a sizable number of those who enter the jail and stay for longer periods of time are young adults who should be prime targets for rehabilitation.

Table 3 shows racial and ethnic group status: From 1968 through 1970, the majority of the inmates were and continued to be white. However, there is a pronounced tendency for an increase in the proportion of black inmates. If this trend continues, by 1980, half the inmate population may be black. For example, in 1968, about 27 percent of the persons processed through the jail were black; in 1969, the proportion had climbed to 31.5 percent, and by 1970, to 35.4 percent.

TABLE 3

Selected Racial and Ethnic Groups of a Sample of Persons
Processed Through the County Jail, 1968-70

Race and/or Ethnic Group	1968		1969		1970		Total	
	No.	Percent	No.	Percent	No.	Percent	No.	Percent
White	150	71.8	148	67.6	103	64.0	401	68.1
Black	56	26.7	69	31.5	57	35.4	182	30.9
Spanish speaking	1	0.5	2	0.9	0	0.0	3	0.5
Other or not available	2	1.0	0	0.0	1	0.6	3	0.5
Total	209	100.0	219	100.0	161	100.0	589	100.0

TABLE 4

Racial Composition of Inmates in the County
Jail, Typical Day, December, 1970

Status	Blacks		Whites		Total	
	No.	Percent	No.	Percent	No.	Percent
Awaiting court action	66	57.9	56	65.1	122	61.0
Awaiting sentence	13	11.4	8	9.3	21	10.5
Under sentence	14	12.3	12	13.9	26	13.0
On work release	0	0.0	4	4.7	4	2.0
Juveniles	21	18.4	6	7.0	27	13.5
Total	114	100.0	86	100.0	200	100.0

However, on a typical day, the racial composition is different.
Table 4 shows the racial characteristics of the inmate population
on December 28, 1970. Totals may vary a few percentage points
one way or the other, but the over-all groupings should be the same.
Thus, nearly 60 percent in the institution on any one day are black. A
higher proportion of blacks than whites are juveniles. The explanation
for these phenomena go beyond our data, but probably blacks have
more difficulty posting bond, are charged with more serious crimes,
and are more likely to live in Washington, D. C. Undoubtedly, institutional racism is also a factor.

Less than one third of our sample reported being married.
Our data did not always show how many were widowed, separated,
and so forth, and thus probably underrepresent marital status. However, 68.5 percent of the U.S. population over 14 years of age are
married.[1] Our group falls far below this rate. This suggests that
the people who pass through the institution have fragile roots in the
family structure and in their communities. (In this context, during
the interview stage of the study, 46 percent of the individuals we
attempted to interview did not live at the address listed for them;
this is further evidence of a group with fragile roots.)

These data (and other data presented later) suggest that efforts
to locate detention centers in inmates' home neighborhoods will not

TABLE 5

Reported Employment Status of a Sample of Persons
Processed Through the County Jail, 1968-70

Item	1968		1969		1970		Total	
	No.	Percent	No.	Percent	No.	Percent	No.	Percent
Employed	113	54.0	130	59.4	92	57.2	335	56.9
Students	20	9.6	17	7.7	28	17.4	65	11.0
Housewives	5	2.4	3	1.4	0	0.0	8	1.4
Retired	2	1.0	2	0.9	2	1.2	6	1.0
Unemployed	69	33.0	67	30.6	39	24.2	175	29.7
Total	209	100.0	219	100.0	161	100.0	589	100.0

be particularly productive. Attention would be best directed at lo-
cating centers in zones of high population concentration, where work
is available, and in the general community area where the individuals
live.

Table 5 presents employment status, and Table 6 presents
occupational categories for the study group. First, in terms of employment, slightly more than half the persons arrested from 1968
through 1970 reported they were employed at the time of arrest.
Housewives, students, and retired persons accounted for about 13
percent of those arrested. The remaining persons (about one third
in each year) reported being unemployed at the time of arrest. About
53 percent reported being employed (or a housewife or student) when
interviewed, but less than one quarter reported ever having used the
Maryland State Employment Service. This, of course, does not
mean that all could or should benefit from the employment service.
As noted, nearly six out of ten reported being employed when arrested,
and presumably many of these had been employed on a steady basis.
(Later, we will present data showing that very few of those interviewed had ever used community social services.)

In terms of occupational groups, the majority of persons
arrested worked in the blue-collar categories. For example, over
half listed their occupation as being in the crafts, operatives, service

TABLE 6

Reported Occupational Groups of a Sample of Persons
Processed Through the County Jail, 1968-70

Occupational Group	1968		1969		1970		Total	
	No.	Percent	No.	Percent	No.	Percent	No.	Percent
Professional and Technical	6	2.9	23	10.5	15	9.3	44	7.5
Managers	2	1.0	7	3.2	2	1.2	11	1.9
Clerical and sales	14	6.7	11	5.0	9	5.6	34	5.8
Craftsmen and foremen	52	24.9	58	26.5	35	21.7	145	24.6
Operatives	19	9.1	22	10.1	7	4.4	48	8.1
Service and private household workers	23	11.0	23	10.5	9	5.6	55	9.3
Laborers	21	10.0	18	8.2	21	13.1	60	10.2
Students	20	9.6	17	7.8	28	17.4	65	11.0
Miscellaneous (housewives, military, etc.)	16	7.6	11	5.0	7	4.3	34	5.8
Not given	36	17.2	29	13.2	28	17.4	93	15.8
Total	209	100.0	219	100.0	161	100.0	589	100.0

TABLE 7

Hourly Wage Rates Reported by a Sample of
Former Inmates Interviewed

Hourly Wage Rates	Montgomery County[a]		Prince George's County		Total	
	No.	Percent	No.	Percent	No.	Percent
$1.99 or less	8	12.7	14	33.3	22	21.0
$2.00 to $2.99	24	38.1	11	26.2	35	33.3
$3.00 to $3.99	11	17.5	5	11.9	16	15.2
$4.00 to $4.99	6	9.5	1	2.4	7	6.7
$5.00 or more	8	12.7	5	11.9	13	12.4
Not given	6	9.5	6	14.3	12	11.4
Total	63	100.0	42	100.0	105	100.0

[a]Wages generally in Montgomery County are slightly higher
than in Prince George's County.

industries, or as laborers. However, of great importance to the
design of a social-service program is the fact that over 15 percent
of those processed through the jail did not report an occupation.

One third of the group interviewed earned at least $3.00 per
hour (about $120 per week); slightly less than one third earned less
than $2.00 per hour. These data in Table 7 probably overrepresent
the earnings of the inmate population. The group of former inmates
interviewed were more stable and probably more likely to be employed than those not interviewed. Hence, we think our income
data probably overreport the economic status of former inmates.

Table 8 provides information on the area of residence for persons processed through Prince George's County Jail. The community
of origin has always been a relatively stable factor. For example,
from 1968 through 1970, about two thirds of the persons processed
through the jail lived, in Prince George's County at the time of their
arrest. About 20 percent lived in Washington, D.C. The remaining

TABLE 8

Stated Area of Residence for a Sample of Persons
Processed Through the County Jail, 1968-70

Place of Residence	1968		1969		1970		Total	
	No.	Percent	No.	Percent	No.	Percent	No.	Percent
Prince George's County	137	65.6	152	69.4	95	59.0	384	65.2
Washington D.C.	42	20.1	39	17.8	37	23.0	118	20.0
Other Maryland county	12	5.7	10	4.6	15	9.3	37	6.3
Other state	13	6.2	15	6.8	14	8.7	42	7.1
Not given	5	2.4	3	1.4	0	0.0	8	1.4
Total	209	100.0	219	100.0	161	100.0	589	100.0

TABLE 9

Highest Year Completed in School Reported by
a Sample of Former Inmates Interviewed

Highest Year Completed	No.	Percent
8 or less	19	18.1
9 to 12	65	61.9
13 to 16	16	15.2
Over 16	3	2.9
Not given	2	1.9
Total	105	100.0

13 percent resided in another Maryland county or in another state.
However, as we pointed out earlier, many of these people were highly
mobile. They were not likely to have permanent addresses or ties
to a community in terms of spouses, property ownership, and so
forth.

Military experience of the survey group remained fairly stable
since 1968. Only about 27 percent of the group (considerably below
the average for U.S. males) had had military experience. [2]

In terms of education, few of the group had been to college,
most had some high school, and nearly 20 percent had eight years
or less of schooling. (See Table 9.) However, the same comment
can be made about education as that made about income. Because
our data on education came from interviews and not from the total
inmate population, we think we probably interviewed the more stable
and more highly educated of those who had been processed through
the jail.

Table 10 provides further indication of the lack of ties these
people had with their communities. About two thirds of those interviewed reported they did not own any property, and this included
automobiles.

TABLE 10

Property Ownership Reported by
a Sample of Former Inmates Interviewed

Property Ownership	No.	Percent
No	70	66.7
Yes	35	33.3
Total	105	100.0

CORRECTIONAL AND CRIMINAL EXPERIENCE OF
PERSONS PROCESSED THROUGH
THE COUNTY JAIL

Tables 11 through 19 provide the basic information on correctional and criminal experience of the study group. First, Table 11
summarizes charges placed against the sample of inmates from 1968
through 1970. An examination of this table indicates four trends and
basic conclusions.

First, crimes of violence, especially criminal homicide, aggra-
vated assault (which is reported in Table 11 along with all assault
crimes and represents a small proportion of the total assault crimes),
robbery, and so forth represented a relatively small proportion of the
total charges lodged against persons processed through the jail.

Second, in the three years reported, the largest single category
of charges was civil offenses, which, for the most part, are traffic
cases.

Third, narcotics charges represented a relatively small portion
of the total. However, there is an unmistakable trend of an increasing
proportion of narcotics cases. For example, in 1968, narcotics
arrests represented 1.2 percent of the total. By 1970, this had
climbed to 5.8 percent.

And finally, although drunkenness is no longer considered a
crime, drunkenness represented a major charge and/or problem (at
least from the intake records produced by the jail). For example,
in 1970, drunkenness charges on the intake form represented 9 percent

TABLE 11

Total Charges Placed Against a Sample of Inmates Processed
Through The County Jail, 1968–70

Charge	1968		1969		1970		Total	
	No.	Percent	No.	Percent	No.	Percent	No.	Percent
Criminal homicide	1	0.4	1	0.4	1	0.5	3	0.4
Robbery	4	1.6	7	2.8	3	1.6	14	2.0
Assault	38	15.5	39	15.7	20	10.6	97	14.2
Burglary	5	2.1	3	1.2	11	5.8	19	2.8
Larceny (including auto theft)	16	6.5	26	10.4	15	8.0	57	8.3
Stolen property (buying, receiving, and possessing)	4	1.6	2	0.8	5	2.7	11	1.6
Weapons (carrying and possessing)	5	2.1	4	1.6	8	4.2	17	2.5
Sex offense	1	0.4	1	0.4	2	1.1	4	0.6
Narcotics	3	1.2	9	3.6	11	5.8	23	3.4
Drunkenness (including driving while under the influence)	32	13.1	25	10.0	17	9.0	74	10.9
Liquor laws	2	0.8	3	1.2	1	0.5	6	0.9
Disorderly conduct	32	13.1	29	11.7	7	3.7	68	10.0
Civil offense (including traffic)	69	28.2	64	25.7	63	33.3	196	28.7
All other offenses	33	13.4	36	14.5	25	13.2	94	13.7
Total[a]	245	100.0	249	100.0	189	100.0	683	100.0

[a]If multiple charges were reported, each was counted separately; thus, the total for each year is greater than the sample.

27

TABLE 12

Most Serious Offenses Charged Against Inmates in
the County Jail, Single Day, November, 1970

Most Serious Offense	No.	Percent
Criminal homicide	22	11.4
Forcible rape	11	5.7
Robbery	33	17.1
Assault	10	5.2
Burglary	21	10.9
Larceny	30	15.5
Weapons (possession)	5	2.6
Narcotics	9	4.7
All civil offenses	16	8.3
All other offenses	36	18.6
Total	193	100.0

of the cases, whereas in 1968 (when drunkenness was a crime), drunkenness involved about 13 percent of the charges.

Table 11 does not accurately reflect the charges against inmates in the jail. On the one hand, about 7,000 persons per year (excluding many juveniles) are processed through the jail. As one might suspect, the majority are involved in relatively minor charges, as evidenced in Table 12. These represent civil offenses, disorderly conduct, driving while under the influence of liquor, and other nonviolent charges. Also, Table 11 does not indicate the nature of the over-all population of the jail at any given time. Because the flow through the institution is such that most people stay for short periods of time, those who do stay in the institution for long periods of time are charged with more serious crimes and/or are unable to post bail.

Table 12 summarizes the charges against inmates lodged in the jail for a period of more than 24 hours on a typical day in November, 1970. (As noted earlier, although there is no such day as a typical

TABLE 13

Most Serious Offenses Charged Against Inmates in the County Jail, Single Day,
Selected Weeks, 1969-70

Most Serious Offense	November 1969		February 1970		May 1970		August 1970		November 1970		Total	
	No.	Percent	No.	Percent	No.	Percent	No.	Percent	No.	Percent	No.	Percent
Criminal homicide	2	1.6	0	0.0	4	3.6	12	11.1	17	13.4	35	6.2
Forcible rape	4	3.3	6	6.0	3	2.7	4	3.7	8	6.3	25	4.4
Robbery	31	25.4	29	29.0	31	27.9	24	22.2	28	22.0	143	25.2
Assault	13	10.6	3	3.0	10	9.1	12	11.1	9	7.1	47	8.3
Burglary	19	15.6	15	15.0	19	17.1	20	18.5	17	13.4	90	15.8
Larceny (including auto)	18	14.8	15	15.0	20	18.0	13	12.0	11	8.7	77	13.5
Narcotics	9	7.4	8	8.0	6	5.4	2	1.9	12	9.4	37	6.5
All civil offenses	5	4.1	5	5.0	6	5.4	3	2.8	7	5.5	26	4.6
All other offenses	21	17.2	19	19.0	12	10.8	18	16.7	18	14.2	88	15.5
Total	122	100.0	100	100.0	111	100.0	108	100.0	127	100.0	568	100.0

TABLE 14

Time Spent in the County Jail for a Sample of Persons Processed in 1968-70

Number of Days Spent in Jail	1968		1969		1970		Total	
	No.	Percent	No.	Percent	No.	Percent	No.	Percent
Less than 1	103	49.3	105	48.0	95	59.0	303	51.4
1, but less than 2	56	26.8	48	21.9	25	15.5	129	21.9
2, but less than 5	17	8.1	29	13.2	19	11.8	65	11.0
5, but less than 15	14	6.7	11	5.0	10	6.2	35	6.0
15, but less than 31	6	2.9	8	3.7	8	5.0	22	3.7
31 days and over	7	3.3	16	7.3	4	2.5	27	4.6
Data not available	6	2.9	2	0.9	0	0.0	8	1.4
Total	209	100.0	219	100.0	161	100.0	589	100.0

day, we think the variation from day to day will be slight.) As the
data indicate, most persons are charged with relatively serious
crimes; thus, a higher proportion of each day's population is faced
with charges involving crimes of violence as opposed to the information in Table 11 describing people who move through the jail in a
year's time.

Table 12 summarizes the charges against inmates in the jail on
a single day. Table 13 provides the same data for a longer time
span, one week, and probably reflects the population of the jail more
accurately.

As noted earlier, most persons processed through the jail stayed
for short periods of time. For example, Table 14 notes that slightly
over half (the proportion remained about the same over the years)
stayed for less than 24 hours. These are (as we implied above)
persons charged with minor crimes and especially civil cases, auto-
mobile and traffic offenses, and so forth. Also, these were persons
who were able to arrange for bond. At the other extreme, small
numbers processed through the institution stayed for more than five
days, about 15 percent. This does not mean that the institution
does not house inmates who stay for long periods of time. Table 15
provides data indicating the length of stay for persons in the jail
on a typical day.

TABLE 15

Time Spent in the County Jail
On a Typical Day, November, 1970

Number of Days Spent in Jail from Arrest Date to Sample Date	No.	Percent
3 or less[a]	10	5.2
4 to 6	11	5.7
7 to 10	6	3.1
11 to 30	56	29.0
31 to 60	33	17.1
61 to 90	24	12.4
91 or more	53	27.5
Total	193	100.0

[a]Inmates in this category are probably undercounted because
many are incarcerated for such a short period of time that they are
not included in the above count.

TABLE 16

Stated Number of Times Arrested for a Sample of Persons Processed
Through the County Jail, 1968–70

Number of Arrests per Inmate	1968		1969		1970		Total	
	No.	Percent	No.	Percent	No.	Percent	No.	Percent
1 (this time)	177	84.7	189	86.3	138	85.7	504	85.6
2	20	9.5	19	8.7	19	11.8	58	9.9
3	10	4.8	8	3.6	1	0.6	19	3.2
4 or 5	1	0.5	2	0.9	3	1.9	6	1.0
6 or more	1	0.5	1	0.5	0	0.0	2	0.3
Total	209	100.0	219	100.0	161	100.0	589	100.0

In terms of time in the institution, the jail seems to have two major population groups. First, there are those who move in and out within about twenty-four hours. These are persons charged with relatively minor crimes and who are able to post bond. At the other extreme are those who stay in the institution for relatively long periods of time. They are serving sentences or are charged with serious crimes, are unable to post bail, or are under sentence. There is some suggestion from the data above that these two groups represent polar extremes; that is, on the one hand, about half the persons processed through the institution are there for less than twenty-four hours; there are few in a middle group who stay from three or four days to two weeks. The other extreme represents those who stay in the institution for thirty days or more.

According to data supplied by inmates as they were processed through the jail, few said they had previous correctional experience. (See Table 16.) Nearly 86 percent claimed they had never before been arrested. However, of the remainder, about 5 percent admitted to three or more arrests. The actual arrest experience of this group of former inmates is probably higher than our data indicate, because the information supplied was provided by inmates and was not checked against any official records. This argument is supported by the interview data.

During the interviews (when it was possible to probe respondents), only 29.5 percent claimed one arrest. (See Table 17.) Also, during the interviews, about 50 percent said they were first arrested before they were 19 years of age.

TABLE 17

Number of Previous Arrests Reported by a Sample of
Former Inmates Interviewed

Number of Previous Arrests	No.	Percent
1	31	29.5
2	20	19.0
3 to 5	22	21.0
Over 5	23	21.9
Not given	9	8.6
Total	105	100.0

There are two major factors that determine the availability of inmates for rehabilitative programs. First, there are the charges placed against them while in jail. Presumably, the more serious charges imply greater security problems, and while this is not necessarily true, most jail personnel tend to assume it is. The second factor is the amount of time people spend in jail. These problems were examined in two different ways.

First, we presented data summarizing the time spent in jail by a sample of inmates from 1968 through 1970. In addition, we presented similar data on the offenses with which the inmates were charged during the same time period. These data are useful in terms of inmate flow within the institution. However, they are less useful in providing a specific picture of the population of the jail during given time periods. Table 18 presents the length of time inmates spent in the jail during selected weeks. We noted elsewhere that the overwhelming majority of persons who move through the jail are short termers and stay less than 24 hours. Because these people are in and out so quickly, they represent a large number of all inmates processed but a small proportion of a given day's population. As the data indicate, a large proportion of the population in the jail at any one time are persons who have been there for relatively long periods of time. For example, nearly two thirds of the jail's population on a typical day are persons who have been in the institution more than 30 days. An additional one quarter are persons who have been in the institution for 10 to 30 days. These data suggest that the institution does house inmates for relatively long periods of time, at least long enough to begin rehabilitative programs.

In terms of the offenses charged against inmates on a typical day, charges ranged considerably. Although the largest category was robbery, it represented about 17 percent of the total. Criminal homicide and forcible rape, relatively hard crimes, also represented about 17 percent of the total. The remaining charges ranged from civil offenses to narcotics, larceny, and so forth. Generally speaking, most inmates in the institution on a typical day were being held on relatively major charges.

Table 19 indicates what happens to a group of persons following their contact with the county jail. In the past three years studied, the largest proportion of inmates were able to post bond—nearly 6 out of 10 fall into this category. Almost one fifth of those processed through the jail were transferred or sentenced to another institution. The number who went to either the Maryland State Department of Correctional Services or to another state institution and the proportion of those who served time in the local institution was about the same, approximately 5 percent to 6 percent of the total group. About 10

TABLE 18

Time Spent in the County Jail Reported by Inmates, Single Day,
Selected Weeks, 1969-70

Number of Days Spent in Jail	November 1969		February 1970		May 1970		August 1970		November 1970		Total	
	No.	Percent	No.	Percent	No.	Percent	No.	Percent	No.	Percent	No.	Percent
Less than 1	0	0.0	2	2.0	1	0.9	0	0.0	3	2.4	6	1.1
1, but less than 5	4	3.3	9	9.0	8	7.2	9	8.3	6	4.7	36	6.3
5, but less than 10	12	9.8	2	2.0	10	9.0	8	7.4	9	7.1	41	7.2
10, but less than 20	10	8.2	31	31.0	11	9.9	9	8.3	10	7.9	71	12.5
20, but less than 30	12	9.8	17	17.0	14	12.6	14	13.0	13	10.2	70	12.3
30, but less than 60	36	29.5	24	24.0	18	16.3	29	26.9	29	22.8	136	23.9
60, but less than 90	19	15.6	6	6.0	27	24.3	18	16.7	20	15.8	90	15.9
90 or more	29	23.8	9	9.0	22	19.8	21	19.4	37	29.1	118	20.8
Total	122	100.0	100	100.0	111	100.0	108	100.0	127	100.0	568	100.0

34

TABLE 19

Postjail Experience for a Sample of Persons Processed Through
the County Jail, 1968-70

Item	1968		1969		1970		Total	
	No.	Percent	No.	Percent	No.	Percent	No.	Percent
Posted bond or collateral	120	57.4	132	60.3	86	53.4	338	57.4
Not guilty and/or dismissed	9	4.3	12	5.5	8	5.0	29	4.9
Transferred to State of Maryland correctional facility	11	5.3	14	6.4	4	2.5	29	4.9
Transferred to other jurisdiction (state, county, federal)	13	6.2	12	5.5	8	5.0	33	5.6
Transferred to Maryland State Institution other than correctional	12	5.7	6	2.7	16	9.9	34	5.8
Released at court	23	11.0	18	8.2	19	11.8	60	10.2
Probation and/or suspended sentence	7	3.4	9	4.1	8	5.0	24	4.1
Served time	10	4.8	15	6.8	12	7.4	37	6.3
Not available	4	1.9	1	0.5	0	0.0	5	0.8
Total	209	100.0	219	100.0	161	100.0	589	100.0

percent had their case dismissed in court, and about 5 percent were found not guilty, apparently in court.

USE OF SOCIAL SERVICES

During the course of the interviews, former inmates were asked if they had ever participated in or used a variety of social services in any way (however superficial). Most popular in terms of use were social security, legal services, and mental-health services. Very low were job training, counseling, and rehabilitation programs. (See Table 20.)

CRIMINAL COURT ACTIVITY

Let us now turn to data on this scope, nature, and over-all drift of court activity in the county. Generally, these data indicate increasing activity in the criminal court field with criminal cases growing at a much more rapid rate than other cases. Also, in terms of juvenile cases, there is a marked growth in the number of cases and the complexity of the problems.

Table 21 provides trend data on criminal cases tried in Prince George's County from 1960 through 1970. In 1960, the county accounted for some 5 percent of the criminal cases tried in Maryland; by 1969-70, the proportion had climbed to 7.2 percent of the total. At the same time, the number of cases in the county more than doubled from 506 in 1960-61 to more than 1,000 in 1969-70. (As noted later, especially in terms of over-all growth and population within the county, there is no reason to expect that this trend will diminish.)

Tables 22 and 23 present data in terms of juvenile cases terminated and ultimate disposition of the cases. As we noted with regard to criminal cases, the county experienced substantial growth in the 1960's. The county's growth rate was much greater than the state as a whole; the same trend is evident for juvenile cases terminated in the state. By 1970, the county produced over 20 percent of the total cases (or 3,873 of 18,292 cases). At the same time, within the county, the number of juvenile cases terminated grew from about 1,200 in 1960 to more than 3,800 in 1970, an increase of over 300 percent.

TABLE 20

Social and Rehabilitative Services Used as Reported by
a Sample of Former Inmates Interviewed

Service Used	Percent
Adult education	11.4
Aid to dependent children (ADC)	5.7
Alcohol treatment	7.6
Correspondence courses	4.8
Credit counseling	2.9
Family counseling	3.8
General education development	8.6
Job training	14.3
Legal aid	24.8
Mental health services	23.8
Narcotics treatment	9.5
Planned parenthood	1.0
Postnatal care	2.9
Prenatal care	2.9
Public library	21.9
Public speaking	6.7
Public welfare programs (excluding ADC)	13.3
Reading and speech	8.6
Religious counseling (services, etc.)	15.2
Social Security	38.1
Vocational rehabilitation	8.6
Youth counseling	6.7
Other	7.7
None	13.3

TABLE 21

Criminal Cases Tried in the County, Selected Years, 1960-70

| Year | Prince George's County | | State of Maryland |
	Number	Percent of State Total	
1960-61	506	5.0	10,117
1965-66	736	6.7	11,048
1969-70	1,055	7.2	14,642

TABLE 22

Juvenile Cases Terminated, 1960-70

| Year | Prince George's County | | State of Maryland |
	Number	Percent of State Total	
1960-61	1,216	9.5	12,819
1961-62	1,602	12.5	12,833
1962-63	2,195	14.1	15,540
1963-64	2,242	13.3	16,884
1964-65	2,237	1.3	17,814
1965-66	2,737	14.8	18,472
1966-67	3,527	18.5	19,109
1967-68	3,865	22.1	17,521
1968-69	3,216	17.3	18,552
1969-70	3,873	21.2	18,292

TABLE 23

Disposition of Juvenile Cases in Prince George's County, 1966-69

Disposition	1966-67		1967-68		1968-69	
	No.	Percent	No.	Percent	No.	Percent
Jurisdiction waived	62	1.8	54	1.4	30	0.9
Charge not sustained	278	8.1	561	14.5	395	12.3
Charge sustained	1,265	36.9	988	25.6	797	24.8
Probation	729	21.3	795	20.5	829	25.8
Institutional commitment	312	9.1	239	6.2	253	7.9
Commitment to public and/or private agency	317	6.3	308	8.0	319	9.9
Other disposition	558	16.3	920	23.8	587	18.2
Sentence suspended	6	0.2	0	0.0	6	0.2
Sentenced	0	0.0	0	0.0	0	0.0
Total	3,527	100.0	3,865	100.0	3,216	100.0

TABLE 24

Time Spent Awaiting Trial for Criminal Cases Tried, 1966-69

Number of Months Spent Awaiting Trial	1966-67				1967-68				1968-69			
	Prince George's County		State of Maryland		Prince George's County		State of Maryland		Prince George's County		State of Maryland	
	No.	Percent	No.	Percent	No.	Percent	No.	Percent	No.	Percent	No.	Percent
Less than 1	187	23.3	2,401	22.4	266	25.5	2,125	18.0	195	21.7	1,492	11.1
1, but less than 2	269	33.5	2,809	26.2	386	37.0	2,919	24.7	377	41.9	2,254	16.7
2, but less than 3	98	12.2	1,682	15.7	132	12.7	2,014	17.0	120	13.3	2,409	17.9
3, but less than 4	72	9.0	1,118	10.5	67	6.4	1,301	11.0	71	7.9	1,782	13.2
4, but less than 5	52	6.5	698	6.5	65	6.2	901	7.6	50	5.5	1,422	10.5
5, but less than 6	28	3.5	491	4.6	38	3.7	499	4.2	24	2.7	971	7.2
6 or more	96	12.0	1,504	14.1	89	8.5	2,076	17.5	63	7.0	3,152	23.4
Total	802	100.0	10,703	100.0	1,043	100.0	11,835	100.0	900	100.0	13,482	100.0

Disposition of Juvenile Cases

First, more than half of the charges were sustained, or juveniles were placed on probation for each year from 1966-67 through 1968-69. Nearly 20 percent of the juveniles were committed to either public or private institutions. There are some discernible trends over the years.

First, there seems to be a strong increase in the number of cases that result in charges not being sustained: In 1966, 8.1 percent of the juvenile cases resulted in charges not sustained; by 1968-69, the proportion had climbed to 12.3 percent of the total. On the other hand, the charges sustained declined by about the same proportion that the charges not sustained increased; in other words, in 1966, about 37 percent of the charges were sustained, while in 1967-68 and in 1968-69, about 25 percent fell into that category. There is a slight tendency for an increase in the number of juveniles placed on probation while the proportions committed have stayed about the same. (See Table 23.)

An important factor concerning the kinds of rehabilitation programs that are possible and needed relates to the age of criminal cases tried in the county and/or the length of time it takes to bring a case to trial. All things being equal, the longer a person awaits trial, the more time he might devote to rehabilitation programs. About 25 percent of the cases in the county come to trial within a month of the person's arrest. At the other extreme, about one in ten cases (7 percent of the cases in 1968-69) require six months or more before the case is tried. The data in Table 24 indicate that about three out of ten persons processed through the county system wait three months or more for trial. This suggests that there is considerable time for many inmates to participate in social-service programs.

NOTES

1. U.S. Bureau of the Census, Statistical Abstract of the United States, 1970, 91st edition (Washington, D.C.: U.S. Government Printing Office, 1970), p. 26.

2. According to information supplied by the Veterans' Administration, Information Office (Washington, D.C., February, 1971), about 44 percent of the male population 18 years and over in the United States are veterans.

4

BASIS
AND CHARACTERISTICS
OF THE
MODEL PROGRAM

In Part I, we discussed the justification and the need for social-service programs in the Prince George's County detention and correctional process. The basic argument and the case is simple. In the early 1970s, about 7,000 persons passed through the jail annually. This number will probably increase to between 9,000 and 13,000 by 1980. Many of these persons not only have legal problems, but personal, social, and physical problems. The jail as structured in the early 1970s functioned almost completely as a custodial and holding institution for the courts. This, in part, is as it should be, but in addition, it should provide a wide range of social and rehabilitative services. The general objective of these services should be to view the jail (or, as the new institution will be called, the detention center) as an opportunity for the provision of social services at the point where the individual first meets the correctional system.

This chapter provides a transition between Part I and Part II: Part I describes the problems; in Part II, we provide a program to meet the problems. This chapter presents the over-all objectives for the program in terms of program goals, facility goals, the ideal inmate flow process needed to maximize benefits from the social-service program, and desired priorities for the program. The chapters that follow provide the detailed plan. (Figure 2 illustrates the scope of programs that will be available.)

PROGRAM GOALS

The detention center should provide a wide variety of social, rehabilitative, and correctional programs that meet certain objectives.

FIGURE 2

Possible Learning Schemes in the Social-Service
Center Programs

Group Size	Activity	Individual Role	Place	Remarks
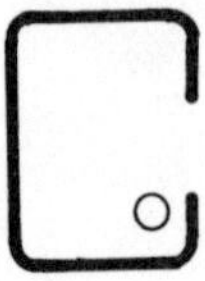 (1)	Reading Film Strips Records Computers Tapes Television Writing Counseling Special Projects Operating Equipment	Active	Social-Service Center	Learning Influenced by Personal Needs and Orientation
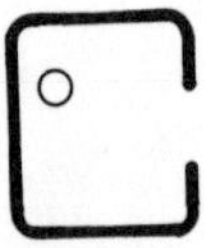 (1)	Listening Reading Writing	Active to Passive	Individual Cell or Anywhere in Institution	Learning Influenced by Individual Needs and Status
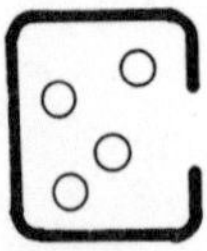 (3)	Seminars Counseling Films Special Projects	Active to Passive	Social-Service Center	Learning Influenced by Varied Situations
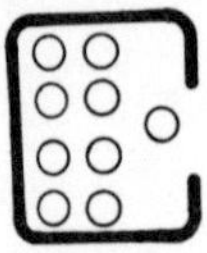 (7)	Discussions Lectures Appearances Movies Demonstrations	Active to Passive	Social-Service Center	Learning Influenced by Varied Situations
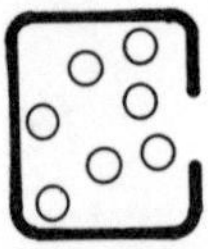 (5)	Operating Equipment Checking Doing Testing	Active	Job Training Facility	Job Training and Learning Influenced by Aptitudes
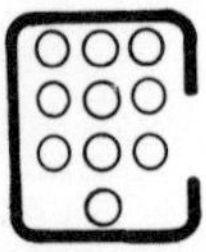 (7)	Operating Equipment Checking Practicing	Active	Job Training Facility	Work Sample Opportunities
 Any Combination	Any of the Above	Active to Passive	Within the Metropolitan Area	Education and Work Release; Community Based Treatment Facility

Given time in the institution and motivation, each inmate should be able to receive diagnostic, rehabilitative, and social services. Then, each should be referred to suitable services upon transfer to another institution or upon release.

Aside from these general goals, the program goals should include the following:

1. Operate an intake process that is oriented toward correctional as well as judicial objectives.

2. Develop and operate a program of social services that involves the broader community in policy, advisory, planning, and cooperative roles. Specifically, the following should be included:

  a. The detention center should have a social-service advisory committee that meets frequently to advise the administration with regard to the effectiveness of social services in the institution and to assist the institution in improving services and receiving broader support from the community.

  b. The advisory committee should contain representatives from social-service agencies, inmates and former inmates, private citizens, and county officials.

  c. The social-service programs in the detention center should be operated by ongoing agencies and institutions under the administration of the Sheriff's Office. This will avoid duplication of programs when services are already available, bring to bear the expert knowledge, services, and funds that are available in the community, and develop responsibility and commitment on the part of ongoing agencies.

  d. The jail and the detention center should make extensive use of volunteers in a variety of categories including but not limited to tutoring, arts and crafts, education, training, and so forth.

3. Social-service programs should be linked to a concept of confinement which is problem- and individual-oriented and makes distinctions at least along these basic lines:

  a. Alcoholics and drug cases.

  b. Juvenile cases.

    c. Inmates with health problems, such as diabetes.

    d. Inmates who are potentially dangerous and those who are not.

    e. The sentenced vs. the unsentenced individual.

    f. Community work and training programs or halfway houses vs. programs in the institution.*

    g. The casual, one-time, or infrequent inmate vs. the frequent inmate.

    h. Inmates charged with relatively minor offenses vs. those charged with serious offenses.

    4. A wide range of services should be available such as the following:

    a. Physical, social, emotional, and educational rehabilitation.

    b. Education, training, and job placement.

    c. Referral of individuals to the next step whether it be a community-based agency or another institution.

    d. Entertainment and recreation.

    e. Counseling services.

    5. Provide an intake process that not only gathers basic data on inmates' correctional problems, but also includes the following:

    a. Produces information that can be used in developing a social-service program for individual inmates while in the institution and followup upon leaving the institution.

    b. Becomes the start of a case file that can move with inmates to the next step in the correctional or institutional setting.

---

*Community-based treatment programs, commonly called "halfway houses," are facilities in the community where residents (in this case, inmates) live under the supervision of a professional staff who administers the program and provides counseling and job assistance.

    c. Is an aid in the management-information system for the detention center which enables the staff to plot and evaluate inmate flow, inmate characteristics, classify inmates in terms of security, evaluate the kinds of services needed, and so forth.

    6. Start the diagnostic and social-service process as soon as possible upon contact with the system. It will be necessary to establish priorities in terms of who should receive services and the kind and amount of services that can be provided. As a general rule, the longer a person is in the institution, the more intensive and thorough should be the diagnostic and treatment programs.

    7. Provide a social-service program integrated with the reception and diagnostic process in the institution, with the classification system in the Maryland Department of Correctional Services, and with the procedures of the state probation and parole unit.

    8. Provide social-service programs from the diagnostic to the treatment process which are voluntary, stress individualized programs, and do not interfere with the courts.

    9. Make maximum use of such new ideas in the correctional field as presentence release, halfway houses, and work and education release.

    10. Maximize on-the-job training opportunities for inmates.

    11. Reflect the atmosphere of the outside world. In this sense, programs should fulfill two objectives:

    a. Provide a transition to the outside.

    b. Be sufficiently attractive and appealing to motivate inmate participation.

    12. Aim at providing social services, skills, information, knowledge, and motivation.

    13. Develop rewards for inmates who apply themselves and do better than might be expected in the programs. The court and probation officials, especially in presentence investigation activities, should be aware of the extent to which inmates are performing at better than expected rates.

14. Encourage the staff of the detention center to use the service of the educational programs, especially in two areas:

    a. In-service training. Regular in-service training should be held for all staff within the institution and in special program at the community college.

    b. Informal conferences and lectures in the detention center.

FACILITY GOALS

The program goals described above should be carried out in the social-service center within the proposed detention center. We use the phrase, "social-service center," to describe a suite of rooms similar to those in the plans for the detention center referred to as classrooms, library, and so forth. The center should be an identifiable unit in the institution and meet certain goals:

1. Produce a facility that is noninstitutional in appearance, form, and decor.

2. Produce a one-stop center that houses all social-service activities in the institution for inmates, staff, and the public.

3. Provide for a variety of services:

    a. Individualized programs for browsing and individual learning.

    b. Individualized counseling and testing programs.

    c. Small group counseling sessions for two to three individuals.

    d. Discussion group programs for five to twenty individuals.

    e. Remote control services to locations within the institution.

    f. Large meetings for up to fifty persons. With the exception of large meetings, it should be possible to offer several combinations of the above services at any one time.

4. Make maximum use of learning technology now and in the future.

IDEAL INMATE FLOW PROCESS

The inmate flow process within the detention center should stress three basic goals: First, it should deflect, as early as possible, as many inmates as is possible from the detention system. This, of course, must be consistent with public safety, medical and court needs, and so forth.

Second, the detention center should provide several levels of correctional services and programs. For example, at one extreme, it might be necessary to provide for a small number of maximum security inmates. Then, moving down the security continuum, the next level might be a fairly small number of moderate security inmates, the next level might be a relatively open environment for a large number of minimum security inmates. This would be followed by the work-release program with participants living in the institution. Finally, there would be the halfway house.*

And third, as a general rule, separate provisions should be made for inmates with the following characteristics:

1. Inmates involved in traffic violations should be processed and handled differently from those charged with criminal offenses.

2. Drug and alcohol cases should be treated separately and differently from criminal cases.

3. Youth, especially those involved in relatively minor problems such as runaways, traffic cases, and the like, should be treated differently and separately from youth involved in serious offenses and who have been in the institution on more than one occasion. Support and family problems should be treated differently from criminal activities.

----

*It was not part of our study to estimate the existing or future levels of security and/or correctional services required. However, we think the following are reasonable estimates of the proportion of inmates who will require given levels of security: maximum security, 15 to 20 percent; medical or observation, 0 to 5 percent; moderate security and minimum security, 20 to 25 percent each; work release and/or trustees, 15 to 20 percent; weekenders and so forth, 5 to 10 percent; and halfway house, 10 to 15 percent.

The Appendix presents our conception of an ideal inmate flow process as compared to the flow in the early 1970s. The basic aim of a rationalized inmate flow process should be to hold in the institution those most in need of custody and to provide the kind of social services inmates need.

OPTIMUM LEVELS AND KINDS OF SERVICES

Four factors will determine the level and kinds of services that inmates are provided in the center. They are the attitudes of staff, the courts, and so forth; available resources; motivation of individual inmates; and the length of time that inmates spend in the detention center.

The negative features of these factors can be minimized in several ways. First, there are staff attitudes and policy decisions. It will be necessary to operate the social-service program with maximum involvement from the county government, the judicial system, and the community. Goals, procedures, and policies should be set and approved by a community-based advisory committee to the social-service center. In addition, there should be extensive training programs for detention center staff, probation and parole staff, the judiciary, and so forth.

Second, there are resources. Insofar as is possible, social services in the detention center should be provided by ongoing agencies within the community. This will make it possible to use many existing services in the county without significantly increasing the cost to the detention center. In other words, if the county board of education can provide education and training, it should be able to do this without a significant increase in the total cost.

Third, in terms of motivation of inmates to use the services of the detention center, various factors should be taken into account. The detention center should be clearly viewed by all persons—staff, inmates, court officials, probation officials, and so forth—as a detention center and not as a jail. The atmosphere should be oriented toward rehabilitation and correction and not punishment. The staff should use every opportunity to define problems, provide information, and direct inmates to services within the institution. For example, immediately upon reception in the center, part of the reception process should be concerned with increasing the likelihood of inmates volunteering to use social-service activities. However, a major and perhaps the most important factor in terms of use of social services in the center will be motivation of the inmates. And this will be a serious problem because inmates coming to the detention center are not apt to view use of the social-service program as their primary need and/or interest. Undoubtedly, the overwhelming majority of persons will be primarily preoccupied with getting out of the institution.

Fourth, there is the factor of time in the detention center. This also will be a major factor in terms of utilization of services. Inmates who spend only a few hours in the center are not likely to make much use of the services. However, even in these cases, it should be possible to provide at least minimal information to many people who pass through the center for a few hours. For example, the intake process should determine whether or not inmates are employed, have serious health problems, and so forth. All inmates leaving the institution could be given a packet of information assembled from brochures, and so forth, supplied by the department of employment security, the department of health, and other pertinent agencies. This information should encourage former inmates who are unemployed to visit the employment service, seek counseling and use similar services. Also, if representatives of the various social-service agencies are available in the detention center, they should offer their services to all persons regardless of the length of time they spend in the institution.

However, as a practical matter, the detention center should aim at providing services to inmates who are in most need of services and those who are there for the longest periods of time. The latter also will probably be those most in need of services.

5

In Chapter 4, we discussed the general goals and objectives for social-service programs and the facility (the social-service center) that should house the programs. This chapter describes the programs that should be offered in the center, over-all content, staffing patterns, and cost estimates. We may leave the implication in this chapter that these programs will be segmented and isolated from each other. This should not be the case: Programs should be offered on an integrated basis.

Chapter 6 describes the organization of social-service center programs, and Chapter 7 describes how the center should be structured. The basic principles of the center should be to offer an integrated range of programs that are available to anyone in the institution (staff and inmates alike) and to use ongoing agencies in the community to staff and conduct the programs which will be administered by the detention center staff.

EDUCATIONAL SERVICES

Principles, Activities, and Goals

Educational programs in the detention center should provide remedial and educational services to interested inmates or staff and especially to inmates in the institution for more than one month. The guiding principles for education programs are described below.

Individualized Learning Programs

Individuals should be able to have an educational prescription developed for them and to follow this program throughout their stay in the institution. The approach, insofar as it is possible, should stress programed instruction and other methods which permit individual study. This will serve two purposes. A large number of persons can be enrolled at a variety of levels. Furthermore individuals can pursue programs without regard to confinement, on the basis of their own interests and inclinations, i.e., in their cells, in day rooms, in the evening, and so forth.

Nongraded Programs

Programs should stress nongraded activities and aim at providing general levels such as General Educational Development (GED) certificates, sufficient education to enable the person to become a bricklayer apprentice, and so forth.

Flexible Enrollment Policies

Because of the constant influx of inmates in the institution, it should be possible for inmates to move in and out of education programs on a daily basis. For example, in some cases it will be necessary to design an educational prescription for a person who may be in the institution for a year and for this person to pursue the prescription throughout his confinement.* In other cases, a prescription will be required for a person who may be in the institution for only a few weeks and may want to continue the program outside the institution upon release.

Accommodate a range of interests,
capacities, and motivations

For example, many prisoners will be functioning at the lower elementary grades in basic educational subjects. Educational services must be able to accommodate them. At another level, some inmate/students will want a GED certificate. The program should be able to provide this. At still another level, some inmates will want to acquire sufficient education to enable them to become apprentices. Again, the program should accommodate them.

---

*For a definition of "prescription," see "The Prescription of Services," Chapter 6.

Basic Areas of Operation

Educational services should focus on the enrollment goals described below, with some cautions. These are duplicating slots or openings, and thus include one individual who may be enrolled in basic education (for one year, for example) and ten others who may be in the programs for brief periods. Also, an individual may be in more than one program. (See Table 25.)

Furthermore, programs should make maximum use of programed instruction and enable the individual to proceed at his own pace and on an individual basis in his cell as well as in a group setting in the social -service center.

Informal Programs. Informal programs should consist of public speaking, community relations, current events, race relations, and similar programs. They should be offered throughout the day or evening at times convenient to groups of interested inmates.

Basic Education. Many inmates will, for all practical purposes, be functionally illiterate. A major emphasis of the programs should be to provide basic education in such areas as reading, mathematics, and language arts, for these persons. The goals will vary depending on inmate needs. In some cases, learning how to complete an application form will be reasonable. In other cases, the goals may be more ambitious.

General Educational Development. Many inmates will have an elementary school certificate and lack a year or so of school to be eligible for a high school diploma. The education program should provide the GED certificate for qualified inmates.

English for the Foreign Born. Increasingly, the county can expect to have more Spanish-speaking inmates who will want to acquire an ability to speak, write, and converse in English.

Speech Therapy. The program should provide opportunities for persons who need training in speech therapy.

Link to Community Efforts

Insofar as possible, when an individual enrolls in a program, the program should be developed along lines similar to programs on the outside. For example, when a prescription is designed for an inmate in GED, care should be taken to make it possible for the

TABLE 25

Basic Education Enrollment Goals, 1975-85

Program	1975		1980		1981-85	
	Minimum	Maximum	Minimum	Maximum	Minimum	Maximum
Informal	40	50	60	80	80	125
Basic education	10	15	20	30	30	40
General educational development (GED)	5	10	10	15	15	20
English for the foreign born	3	5	5	10	10	15
Speech therapy	3	5	5	10	10	15
Total	61	85	100	145	145	215

inmate to transfer to a program on the outside should he leave the
institution.

Testing

All inmates should be tested (on a voluntary basis) in educational
achievement and development no later than the fifth day of incarceration.
On the basis of these tests, it will be possible to design an educational
prescription. If inmates who have been in the institution less than five
days wish and request the tests, testing should not be denied them.

Innovation

The physical development of the social-service center should
be such that when educational innovations occur in the future, the
institution should, with little or no difficulty, be able to adjust to them.

Materials and Equipment

The educational programs should have the following equipment
and materials:

Materials and Equipment	Estimated Cost
1. Basic curricula and materials in reading	$1,500
2. Basic curricula and materials in mathematics	1,500
3. Basic curricula and materials in language and study skill development	1,000
4. World of Work program and curricula	900
5. GED program and curricula	200
6. Consumer-education program and curricula	1,500
7. Study carrels equipped with electrical systems, intercom, tape-listening components, daylight movie screens, tape unit structured for earphone jacks, intercom switch, etc. (20 @ $500)	10,000
8. Teaching machines that should be available from the Federal Bureau of Prisons (20 @ $1,000)	20,000
9. Language masters (5 @ $300)	1,500
10. Miscellaneous	5,000

Because of space limitations in the existing county jail, it is not feasible to launch the educational programs until the new institution is available. (We assume this will be about 1975.) Thus, the purchase of educational equipment will be deferred until then. We assumed a three-phase implementation: a very limited program in 1971, a fairly extensive program in 1975, and the completion of the program in 1980. During the first phase, the center expected to invest about $7,000 in educational materials, equipment, and supplies—essentially portions of items 1 through 6 for the present jail and community-based treatment center and materials for staff training. During the second and third phases, approximately $40,000 should be spent bringing the program to full strength by purchasing the remainder of items 1 through 6 and items 7 through 10. Detailed cost estimates for each phase are in Chapter 8.

Portions of items 1 through 6, and 10 will have to be replaced approximately every other year. Items 7, 8, and 9 are one-time expenses.

RECREATIONAL SERVICES

Recreational programs and activities should be a part of the center. These programs should serve basic purposes: (1) provide inmates with opportunities for physical exercise; (2) develop leisure time habits; (3) provide opportunities for intergroup and interpersonal relations; and (4) provide opportunities for motivation and skill development.

In addition, the following programs should be available.

Talent Shows. Inmates can be organized to present periodic talent shows and make presentations before other groups of inmates and the community.

Movies. Commercial and special purpose movies (dealing with social problems, travel, etc.) can be rented and shown periodically in the institution.

Programed Instruction. The programed-instruction machines to be used in the education program can also be used to provide programed instruction in such activities as card games, bridge, driver training, and similar activities.

Debate Clubs. Debate clubs can be organized within the institution to hold periodic sessions before groups of inmates.

Miscellaneous. Recreational programs such as checkers, chess, ping pong, choral groups, and so forth should be available.

Role Playing and Group Therapy. Role-playing sessions can be organized around interpersonal problems such as alcoholism, criminal activity, relations with the police, and similar areas. Groups of inmates can, on a volunteer basis, produce skits for other inmates.

Physical exercise. Most inmates in the institution should be encouraged to engage in physical activities, especially younger inmates. Programs can be designed consisting of running in place, weight lifting, calisthenics, and so forth.

Recreation programs will require extensive use of specialists and/or volunteers (i.e., public speaking teachers, discussion leaders, etc.). Thus, staff costs will be minimal and with the exception of physical activities, this component should be supported by the information-media services program.

INFORMATION-MEDIA SERVICES

In another publication we described in detail a role for institutional library services.[1] These purposes will not be restated here, but it should be clear that a large, well-functioning library and/or media center in a detention center is important for the following reasons.

First, inmates have a great deal of free time which they should be able to spend in reading, listening, and looking and in recreational activities, amusement, acquisition of knowledge and ideas, and similar areas.

Second, libraries are important because inmates live in a constricted setting which is routine and movements are limited. Library services provide an opportunity to gain a sense of the outer world and temporarily leave the restricted setting to roam about the library world with books.

Third, an institutional library program is the major activity in the institution that can be most similar to experiences in the outside community. The individual is able to control his own activities in the library and select what he would like to do at his own pace.

And finally, because inmates will vary in terms of educational functioning level and interests, the library must be more than a collection of books. It should provide information-media services (IMS) whereby individuals are able to gain information, ideas, and so forth, from a variety of sources including books, records, and audio-visual equipment.

We propose that more than traditional library services be of-fered in the detention center and that the library be the focal point for all information services in the center. Hence, we describe library services as IMS.

Basic Principles

IMS in the detention center should be the major focal point of the social-service center for numerous reasons. Administration of IMS should follow procedures that govern public library services in the county. It should not be necessary to follow exact procedures in terms of circulation, cataloging books, and so forth. However, IMS should be managed in such a way that inmates become accustomed to libraries from experience in the program in the social-service center.

Materials in the IMS program in the institution should circulate about the institution. Inmates should be permitted and encouraged to check out materials for use in their cells. Also, materials should be stored in the cell blocks as well as in the social-service center.

It will be necessary to develop techniques to motivate inmates to use these services. Various efforts might be tried. Jackets of books and materials available should be displayed within the social-service center or about the institution. Brief descriptions of materials should be distributed to inmates. Books and materials should be dis-played prominently in the cell blocks to encourage use. Also, there should be as few impediments and restrictions as possible for inmates to obtain materials.

Other attempts to encourage IMS use should be in developing small reading groups within the institution, encouraging inmates to recommend titles and materials to be purchased, and consulting in-mates in terms of the usefulness and effectiveness of the IMS pro-gram.

Inmates should participate in IMS through selection and evalu-ation, and in assistance to staff in cataloging, administering, and distributing materials.

The program should be administered as a branch of the county library. The library should have the responsibility for selecting materials, managing and supervising IMS repairing materials, staffing, and providing basic staff supervision. However, all of these activities should be carried out in close cooperation with the administration of the detention center.

IMS should not refuse donated materials but should select and evaluate donated materials carefully. It should avoid building a program largely on relatively obsolete, donated materials such as exist in the present jail. In addition, IMS should not only be the central point within the institution where library materials are stored and circulated, but it should also be the center of activity for all audio-visual equipment and materials.

The IMS program should be so structured that the materials, equipment, and activities of the center benefit all kinds of inmates within the institution, from those in maximum security to those with maximum freedom of movement. This will necessitate innovative ways of circulating materials and equipment, such as frequent movement of materials about the institution to enable inmates confined to their cells to select, read, and listen to materials while in their cell and the storage of materials in convenient places throughout the institution. IMS also should be available to staff as well as inmates.

Materials and Equipment

The following equipment and materials should be part of the IMS program:

Materials and Equipment	Estimated Cost
Books (paperbacks for the most part), approximately 4,000	$6,000
Periodicals (popular, such as Reader's Digest, local newspapers, etc.) (10 @ $5 per year)	50
Reference materials (including legal publications, dictionaries, encyclopedias), 100 items initially	1,500
Motion picture projector (16 millimeter),	600
super-8 cartridge projectors and 20 cartridges	250

Materials and Equipment		Estimated Cost
Video tape system (1)		$2,000
Video tapes	(8 @ $25)	200
File cabinets	(2 @ $125)	250
Cassette tape recorders	(100 @ $50)	5,000
Prerecorded cassette tapes		2,000
Recording Tapes		200
Records		500
Filmstrip viewers	(2 @ $180)	360
Replacement of materials (annually)		5,000
Televisions	(10 @ $300)	3,000
Miscellaneous		2,000

The program should be brought to the above capacity (inventory) by 1980. The total cost of equipping the program described here is about $30,000. Priority for the first phase should go to providing half the books and periodicals, reference materials, shelves, and display cases. When the new institution is completed in 1975, at least half the cassette tape recorders, approximately half the prerecorded cassette tapes, approximately half the records, and the motion picture projector should be available. We estimate that to put the program into operation for the first year, it will cost approximately $5,000. The second phase should cost about $15,000 and the third phase about $10,000. An annual cost of $5,000 will also be required to maintain the program on an ongoing basis for replacement and repair.

INDIVIDUALIZED LEARNING

Most programs in the social-service center should be based on individualized learning procedures. Individuals should be able to stop, start, and involve themselves in programs at their own pace and level. Further, it should be possible for learning to occur anywhere in the institution.

The major mechanism to make this possible should be programed instructional materials and cassette recorders with prerecorded tapes. Inmates should be permitted to take recorders to their cells and pursue programs at their own inclination and leisure. For this reason we recommend the purchase of 100 cassette recorders as well as a large number of prerecorded tapes. In some cases, it will be necessary for volunteers to record tapes for use in the institution.

Also, the social-service center staff should explore the possible use that can be made of the programs carried on the community educational television station. (In Prince George's County, this is Channel 26, WETA.[2])

JOB INFORMATION SERVICES

There should be services within the center that relate to job activities. These services should be primarily for inmates who were unemployed or underemployed when arrested. Priority should go to those who have been in the institution the longest period of time and are about to be discharged. The range of services should focus on four basic areas.

Job Information. The employment service should make available the Job Data Bank currently in use in the Washington metropolitan area. This data-bank material should be available for inmates to examine so that they may identify jobs for which they might be qualified or in which they are interested.

Referral Services. There should be opportunities for inmates upon leaving the institution to be referred to a job, training, or social-service agency.

Special Job Counseling. Many inmates are veterans (or others) eligible or in need of special services. The job placement services within the institution should be able to identify these inmates and provide special services.

Testing and Counseling. Many inmates, especially those who are young and unemployed, have had little contact with the manpower system in the United States. They should have the opportunity to be tested for job interests and aptitudes and to participate in intensive job related counseling programs.

Personnel. The Maryland State Employment Service should assign at least one full-time equivalent to the social-service center. This need not be a single person but a combination of individuals who can provide the services detailed above. The employment service representative should be generally available to persons as they are discharged from the institution, especially on days of heavy traffic, i.e., Mondays, days following holidays, and so forth.

WORK AND EDUCATION RELEASE

In 1969, Prince George's County Commissioners adopted a work-release program to permit inmates "under sentence to be released to work, to seek work, and to participate in training or education programs 'in the county.'" The criteria for eligibility are liberal: An applicant must be employable, not work or seek work around alcoholic beverages, firearms, and so forth, not have serious charges before the courts, or not have prior probation, parole, or work release revoked because of absconding or other problems.

Because the present jail is overcrowded, it does not permit the segregation of inmates on work release from the general population in the institution, and it lacks staff to administer and conduct the work-release program. Thus, the program has only been superficially implemented. In 1970, about four persons were on work release from Prince George's County Jail. Furthermore, some inmates (trustees) are regularly assigned to jobs in the court house and in the jail. For all practical purposes, such persons, especially those working outside the jail, are work releasees.

The work-release program should be implemented along these lines: First, a community-based treatment facility (halfway house) should be established immediately outside the present institution. Most of the current trustees, and up to at least fifteen to twenty-five inmates could be enrolled in this program. Two centers might be established—one in the College Park-Hyattsville area, where, in all probability, most of the participants will work. Also, since most of the trustees work in Upper Marlboro, a similar center should be established in that area.

A work-release program should also be established in the new detention center. In the plans available at the time of this study, a work-release building was indicated in the plans but was to be deferred for several years after the basic structure was completed. The facility was intended to accommodate fifty individuals. If a halfway house is designed to accommodate thirty persons (and this can be flexible because participants can be added as the situation requires), the work-release program would require space for no more than ten to fifteen persons. The work-release program should be an intermediate step before assignment to the halfway house. In other words, the flow of inmates should be first to the work-release program in the institution and then to the halfway house outside the institution.

But the establishment of a community-based treatment center should not be delayed while waiting for the construction of the work-release facility in the new detention center. The halfway house can be established immediately in rented quarters.

The work release and the community-based treatment center programs should have staff to provide these functions and services: administration, job development, and counseling. The staff should administer programs in terms of housekeeping duties, supervision of releasees, and so forth under the general jurisdiction of the detention center's warden. The staff should provide liaison with the state employment service and employers and seek jobs when necessary for persons to be assigned or on work release. And finally, the staff should also provide counseling services on a regular basis to releasees. Counseling should be on a periodic basis and deal with such problems as interpersonal relations, family relations, and similar problems. The staff should work closely with employers, anticipate problems, and counsel employers about relations with releasees as well.

The goal should be to enroll a minimum of 10 to 15 individuals in work-release programs and 20 to 30 in the halfway house to make both programs reasonably economical. If 30 to 45 are enrolled in both programs, the cost per releasee will be approximately $16.00 to $17.00 per day or about $6,000 annually. Enrollees in the program should be expected to compensate for their own board and room which will reduce the cost to the county to approximately $3,000 to $4,000 per individual. (The present cost of operating the jail is approximately $2,600 per inmate.)

Individuals could be assigned to the work-release and halfway-house programs in several ways: First, the courts should have the over-all responsibiltiy of "sentencing" or assigning an individual to a halfway house. This could be the sentence, but the courts should also use the services of probation and parole to evaluate an individual prior to diverting him to a halfway house. In terms of work release, the courts could also assign individuals, but in addition, the Sheriff's office could assign individuals to work release, especially to trustee jobs.

Education-Training Release. The present work-release program will also permit education- or training-release programs (although such efforts are not now underway), that is, release of inmates for the purposes of attending training or education programs. There are two excellent possibilities that should be explored immediately.

First a joint training program could be developed between Prince George's County and Montgomery County for job training. The Federal Manpower Development and Training Act (Section 251) is earmarked for support of training programs for inmates of prisons or jails. It should be possible for both institutions to present a joint proposal to the Maryland State Manpower Coordinator for support of a program for approximately ten inmates from each county. This program would pay not only tuition but all costs of the project including a stipend to the inmate enrollees. The value of this program is that it is specifically designed to provide job training of a short-term nature from a few weeks up to a year.

Second, the county should explore the possibility of seeking support through the Manpower Development and Training Act for on-the-job training for inmates in the detention center or jail. Programs of this sort can also be supported by the Manpower Development and Training Act or conducted with little or no county, state, or federal outlay. Essentially, it is necessary to find an employer who is willing to train inmates on the job. Again, this is a most attractive way of establishing permanent work habits among inmates. Inmate trainees should be assigned definite work and learn specific skills that are necessary in the labor market.

JOB TRAINING IN THE DETENTION CENTER

It is neither possible nor desirable to conduct all job training programs outside the institution. Thus, there is need for a highly flexible training facility on the grounds of the institution. This facility should serve these basic purposes. It should provide training opportunities at any one time for up to about fifteen inmates. The facility should also provide specific kinds of training on a relatively short-term basis for jobs that are open in the community. And finally, because many of the inmates coming through the institution will have had little experience in the work world, the training facility in the institution should also serve as a work sample facility.

A "work sample facility" is designed to provide persons who have had little or no work experience with an opportunity to test their potential, capabilities, interests, and so forth in actual work settings. This is necessary because it has been demonstrated in a variety of ways that regular testing programs are generally inadequate for low-income groups. A work sample program provides an individual with opportunity to test his own interests and use of tools and also enables counselors to test the way in which a person operates in a simulated work setting. This has proved to be a most realistic way of assessing the kinds of work needs a person exhibits.

A prefabricated facility (approximately 60 to 70 feet by 30 to 40 feet) should be located on the grounds of the new detention center. This facility should be equipped with work stations for approximately 15 individuals, a tool crib, sufficient electrical and exhaust outlets, and be so constructed that a variety of different kinds of training programs and facilities may be conducted. For example, the facility should be flexibly developed to allow the conduct of an automotive repair training program; this would replace the welding program, and so forth.

Information at the time of this study supplied by the Maryland State Employment Service indicated that a variety of jobs requiring relatively little training were in great demand in Prince George's County area. Job training should be conducted in these job areas.

HEALTH SERVICES

The aim of the infirmary in the detention center should be to provide emergency care and to maintain medical services in the facility. Persons requiring treatment or consultation would request service from the custodial staff who would post a sick call list. Activities in the infirmary should include fire basic services.

Sick call would take approximately two hours each day and would be conducted by the medical consultant. A twenty-four-hour telephone medical consultation service should be available. Psychiatric evaluation and detoxification treatment should also be available when necessary. In addition, every person who has been in the detention center for twenty-four hours should have an examination that would include a urinalysis and a chest X-ray (both completed at the detention center's laboratory) and a serology for syphilis (completed by the state laboratory).

The physical plant for the infirmary should include a medical office, waiting room, doctor's office X-ray unit with darkroom, medical isolation unit, small laboratory that could be put in the utility room or the darkroom, examination room, and an eight-bed ward.

Personnel should include one medical doctor and hospital corpsmen. The doctor would devote 40 percent of his time (16 hours a week) to the infirmary. His duties would include daily sick call and

24-hour availability for consultation service. His annual salary would be $10,000. Hospital corpsmen would provide general care of patients, general laboratory and X-ray work, and would clean the facilities; two full-time equivalents would each receive an annual salary of $6,000.

Following is a list of necessary equipment.[3]

		Estimated Cost
Materials and Equipment		
Examining Room		
Drug security cabinet		$1,200
Examination table		315
Examination stool		50
Waste receptacle		40
Treatment cabinet		185
Kalon jar set with rack		20
Blood pressure device		50
Stethoscopes (Littmann 30775)	(3 @ $25)	75
Welch Allyn diagnostic set		110
Instrument container		25
Miscellaneous instruments		100
Applicator jar (for swabs)		5
Locked filing cabinet		130
Syringe destroyer (for security)		190
Gooseneck floor lamp		20
Electric wall clock		10
X-ray Equipment		
X-ray machine for bone, skulls, chest (1/60th of a second)		8,000
Darkroom equipment (nonprofessional unit)		1,500
Laboratory Equipment		
Binocular microscope (used)		400
Laboratory stool		35
Centrifuge		150
Ward		
Regular hospital beds (nonpower)	(8 @ $180)	1,440
Chairs	(8 @ $25)	200

Materials and Equipment		Estimated Cost
Night tables	(8 @ $7)	$ 56
Swivel chair		95
Occasional chair		75
Desk (small)		140
Locked file cabinet, 5-drawer		130
Utility cart		40
Electric wall clock		10

IMPLEMENTATION IN
THE EXISTING JAIL

Because the present jail is vastly overcrowded and because funds and staff are not available, next to nothing in the way of social services is available. When this study was conducted, a target date for completion of the new detention center had not been set. In our plans, we assumed that the new center would be available by 1975. To await the completion of the new center before any rehabilitation programs are launched seems inconceivable. In our study, we made specific recommendations for programs that should be implemented immediately. These especially included work-release and halfway-house programs. In addition, efforts should be put underway to provide health services, library services, and informal education to all who need such services and generally to improve the comfort of inmates in the jail. (At this writing, the sheriff had plans to air-condition the jail and construct an exercise yard.)

In Chapter 6, we will discuss the organization and process of programs that should be offered in the social-service center, i.e., how they should operate and relate to each other.

NOTES

1. See Social, Educational Research and Development, Inc., Institutional Library Services: A Plan for the State of Illinois (Chicago: American Library Association, 1970). 110 pages.

2. See WETA/Channel 26, Secondary School Television Service Teacher's Guide, 1970-71 (Washington, D.C.: The Greater Washington Educational Television Association, Inc., 1970). 142 pages.

3. W. K. Wright, Deputy Purchasing Agent, Equipment and Furniture Price List for Use in Preparation of Fiscal Year 1971-72 Capital Outlay Budget Requests (Upper Marlboro, Md.: Budget Department, Prince George's County, Central Purchasing, n.d.), on which our prices for office furnishings are based.

**TECHNICAL AND
MANAGEMENT FEATURES
OF THE
MODEL
SOCIAL-SERVICE PROGRAM**

ORGANIZATIONAL PATTERNS OF ADMINIS-
TRATION AND STAFF

The social-service center program should be under the direction of the social-service center director. This person would report to the warden of the detention center and be on the detention center's staff and payroll. (Minimum qualifications are described later; see "Staff Requirements.")

The major responsibilities of the social-service center director should include the following:

Coordinate, organize, and manage all services in the center.

Insure effective liaison among agencies operating out of the center and between the programs and the detention center staff.

Supervise and train staff and inmate aides working in the center.

Schedule and arrange for programs within the center.

Manage volunteer programs and recruit volunteers.

Evaluate all activities within the center.

Supervise the screening process.

Provide an annual report to the county commissioners through the warden and the sheriff reporting in detail about the program and the number of individuals served.

Seek sources of support for the program.

Serve as secretary to the social-service center advisory committee.

We propose that program personnel (education, library, employment, etc.) be supplied by the respective agencies. (Specific staff needs are discussed in "Staff Requirements.")

THE SOCIAL-SERVICE INTAKE FLOW PROCESS

Detention Center Reception. As part of the routine processing of inmates, all persons received in the detention center would be interviewed by a reception officer. As part of routine processing, this officer would collect basic social, economic, and personal information on each person. This step would be more elaborate and slightly more time consuming than the present intake process and would function to provide the county data processing unit with a basic data bank on all inmates and to provide basic data for the social-service program to identify inmates who were possible participants in the program. *

Copies of the intake forms would be available to

the county data processing unit,

the county detention center files, and

the social-service center files.

As part of the routine processing of entering inmates, the intake officer would briefly describe the services available in the social-service center. Inmates to be released in a short time could then schedule a consultation with the social-service center staff.

---

*This task will require complete revision of the present data collection process during intake. The present process is inefficient, ambiguous, inaccurate, and does not lend itself to data collection and evaluation. Although this goes beyond our study, we recommend that the information process be completely redesigned to collect more accurate and useful information and to store the information in a manner that will make it more usable than at is at present.

Inmates who would probably be detained more than five days could request consultation with the staff within the first five-day period.

Initial Screening. Each morning the social-service center director and the director of the vocational rehabilitation program would interview inmates in consultation. The screening interview should be brief and determine the nature, seriousness, and urgency of the problems faced by the individual; the agency (if any) to which the individual should be referred if he is to be released to the community; the feasibility of a preliminary plan of social services within the institution; and the likelihood of the individual being eligible for vocational rehabilitation services.

It is difficult to estimate the number of persons who might be served in this initial-screening phase. The number would depend almost entirely on how inmates viewed the services. And this would depend on the quality of the services, attitudes of the staff, organization of the program, and so forth. Presently, twenty to thirty inmates are processed each day, most of whom are released within twenty-four hours. We estimate that three to seven persons per day (of those who have been in the institution five days) will avail themselves of an imaginative and effective initial-screening service. If the program becomes effective and popular with inmates, in terms of 1980 inmate population, five to ten persons per day should pass through the initial-screening process.

At this point, the social-service flow will result in so-called streams of overlapping service: the stream managed and conducted by the social-service center staff, the stream managed and conducted by the state vocational and rehabilitation division, individually planned programs, and a miscellaneous stream consisting of referral to various programs. (These are explained below.)

Evaluation, Referral, and Plan of Service. In the case of general, deferred referral, an inmate may be referred to the education representative, the employment service representative, to a specific program within the institution or within the community upon his release, or he may be recommended to a training or counseling program to start at some future date.

Those inmates who appear to meet the eligibility requirements of the division of vocational rehabilitation will be referred to this agency which will have the major rehabilitative responsibilities in the social-service center. We expect this to be the major flow of inmates. And finally, an inmate may plan his own program.

Inmates upon referral should have a plan of service developed for them. This would be a prescription that should consist of a complete diagnostic analysis and recommended program whether the inmate remains in the detention center, is transferred to another institution, or released. This plan, of course, should accompany him when he leaves the detention center.

SCOPE OF SERVICES, INDIVIDUALLY GENERATED
AND PRESCRIPTIVE

Many persons coming through the institution will be there for short periods of time, not be eligible for vocational rehabilitation, not be interested in the services of the social-service center, not know what their needs are, and so forth. These persons will plan their own program which might range from reading one book during their confinement to enrolling in a programed instruction course. They will probably represent the major users (on a man-hour basis) of the social service center.

Other inmates will be eligible and in need of staff services that could range from a few minutes of guidance with a representative of the local employment service, for example, to a complete program developed by the division of vocational rehabilitation and involve many days of professional service.

The process of sorting out inmates into these general streams of participation—individually generated and prescriptive services—is described in the sections that follow.

VOCATIONAL REHABILITATION SERVICES

Inmates who are referred (following the preliminary screening) to the division of vocational rehabilitation for intensive screening and evaluation and who are considered eligible for vocational rehabilitation services will be the responsibility of this unit. (There are three general eligibility requirements: Clients must have a recognized handicap—physical, emotional, etc.; the handicap must be capable of treatment; and there must be a reasonable expectation that the prospective client can be vocationally rehabilitated.) The vocational rehabilitation evaluation staff will conduct the screening process with the assistance of the screening committee and the social-service center director. When appropriate, the evaluation will include a physical, psychiatric testing, survey interview, social and family appraisal, and criminal experience appraisal.

In addition to determining whether or not the individual meets the vocational education eligibility requirements, four factors will be considered: (1) the extent to which court activities may interfere with the proposed program; (2) attitudes and motivations of the individual; (3) whether the needed services can be provided within or without the institution consistent with the court and correctional requirements and the program set for the individual; and (4) the extent to which the individual meets the program priority requirements. Individuals eligible for vocational rehabilitation services should then be provided with a prescription containing programs described in the next section.

THE PRESCRIPTION OF SERVICES

The prescription of services can contain any combination of these components:

1. Job training. Inmates may receive job training within the institution or be referred either to work release or, upon release from the institution, to training facilities on the outside. This component may be preceded by a work-sample phase to be conducted in the job training facility in the social-service center.

2. Physical rehabilitation. Inmates who are in need of physical rehabilitation (surgery, dentures, glasses, tattoo removal, etc.) will be referred to services either in the county department of health or, upon release, to another agency.

3. Personal and social counseling and guidance. This component will consist of guidance and counseling in personal, emotional, and family problems. Again, the services could be provided within the institution or outside the institution depending on the status of the individual.

4. Basic education. Depending on the individual's educational needs, he may be referred to basic education, GED, remedial education, speech therapy, and so forth—again within the institution or outside the institution depending on his status.

5. Welfare services. Eligibility for welfare and other social services will be determined.

6. Follow through. Persons within the institution will be under the supervision of the social-service center director or the vocational rehabilitation coordinator, depending on their status. The respective staff and agencies will have responsibility for all follow through. Upon

discharge from the institution, the vocational rehabilitation administration will have the responsibility for following through on inmate-clients assigned to the program; those not assigned to the program will be followed through by agencies having the major responsibility for their rehabilitation program.

Individuals not eligible for services from the vocational rehabilitation administration and needing services that can be supplied in the social-service center will be provided a prescription and program by the social-service center staff containing similar elements to those in the vocational rehabilitation program.

PRIORITIES FOR SERVICES

The basic aim of the social-service program should be to provide services at least at a diagnostic level for any individual who is interested and motivated, is in need and has no alternative source of support, or will be in the institution long enough to benefit from the services and/or who can be referred to services outside the institution upon release or discharge.

As a practical matter, it will be necessary to establish general priority categories to insure that the most needy persons receive services. We recommend two major groupings and priorities within the major groups. The first group will be those who are eligible for services under the vocational rehabilitation administration. These persons will be those most in need. The second group will be those ineligible for vocational rehabilitation services and will be the group with lesser needs.

Priorities for the Vocational Rehabilitation Administration

Priorities for eligibility in the vocational rehabilitation program will go in descending order to those falling into the following groups: (1) Inmates in the institution more than fifteen days who have had previous convictions and who meet the requirements of the state department of vocational rehabilitation; (2) Inmates who have been in the institution more than fifteen days who do not have previous convictions and meet the requirements of the State Department of Vocational Rehabilitation.

Priorities for the Social-Service Program

Generally, all persons not eligible for the vocational rehabilitation program will be eligible for the general pattern of social services within the institution. Again, as a practical matter, it will be necessary to establish priorities. The priorities may be as follows: (1) Inmates who have been sentenced to thirty days or more in the institution, who may have previous convictions, and do not meet the requirements of vocational rehabilitation; (2) Inmates who have not been sentenced, but have been in the institution for fifteen days or more, have not had prior convictions, and do not meet the requirements of vocational rehabilitation.

Consistent with security, the requirements of the courts, and so forth, all inmates should be permitted maximum use of the social-service center.

PARTICIPATION AND ENROLLMENT PROJECTIONS

Table 26 provides estimates of the use of services and programs through 1985 on a daily basis. These data should be read as estimates. They assume the following: The population of the detention center in 1980 will be between 9,000 and 13,000. The detention center will have a wide range of services and programs ranging from the components discussed in Chapter 5 to a community-based treatment facility. Almost all inmates in the detention center will be able to participate in programs. Considerable overlap should occur, i.e., on any given day an individual may participate in educational programs, recreational programs, and so forth. And finally programs of high quality that have high priority should be offered.

STAFF REQUIREMENTS

The social-service center will require the following staff persons:

Director, social-services center, should be available in 1971. The director should have these qualifications: a master's degree in social work, education, or one of the social sciences; two to three

TABLE 26

Estimate of Daily Enrollments and Participation Projections in the
Social-Service Center, 1975-85

Program	1975		1980		1981-85	
	Minimum	Maximum	Minimum	Maximum	Minimum	Maximum
Initial social-service screening	3	7	5	7	7	10
Vocational rehabilitation screening	2	3	3	5	5	7
Preparation of prescription, vocational rehabilitation	2	3	3	5	5	7
Preparation of Prescription, social-service center	2	3	3	5	5	7
Educational services	61	85	100	145	145	215
Recreational services	50	75	75	100	150	200
Information media services	50	75	75	100	100	125
Job information services	5	10	10	15	10	15
Work educational release	0	0	40	50	40	50
Community-based treatment	20	25	25	30	25	30
Job training	5	10	10	15	10	15
Health services	3	5	5	7	7	10

years of correctional or related experience; experience in two to three
social services such as employment, education, welfare, and so forth;
and two to three years of administrative experience in social services.

This person should be employed at about Prince George's County Pay
Grade 28, [1] with an annual salary of $12,000 to $16,000.

Assistant director, social-service center, should be available
in 1975. This person should be trained and educated in the same
general areas as the social-service center director, although slightly
less education and experience is required. This position should be
filled no later than 1975—perhaps earlier in the event that the program
grows more rapidly than envisioned here. Prince George's County
Pay Grade 26, annual salary, $11,000 to $14,000.

Coordinator, educational services, should be available part-time
in 1975. This person should be assigned to the center by the county
board of education. Generally the coordinator should be experienced
in adult education, the setup, operation, and use of a variety of media
equipment, and be able to function in a correctional situation. He
should have available consultant services from other units and divisions
within the county school system, especially remedial reading, testing
and guidance, and so forth. This position could start as a half-time
assignment in 1975, but by 1980, assuming growth rate as anticipated
here, this position should be full-time. Annual salary, $9,000 to
$15,000.

Social-service counselor, should be available part-time in 1971.
The position will consist of general counseling (personal, family, job,
etc.). Counselors will report to the center's director. This position
should be filled by one half-time equivalent in 1971 and two full-time
individuals by 1975. Prince George's County Pay Grade 18, annual
salary, $7,000 to $10,000.

Coordinator, job and vocational training, should be available
part-time in 1975. This person should be assigned by the county
board of education and be an experienced vocational educator with a
background in manpower training and development. This person should
be able to set up, manage, and supervise the vocational training and
job training facility. The position should be filled on a half-time basis
in 1975, but assuming the program envisioned here, the position should
become full-time by 1980. Annual salary, $9,000 to $15,000.

Coordinator, information media services, should be available
in 1975. This position should be assigned by the county library. The

person should be a professional librarian experienced in adult programs
The coordinator should have over-all responsibility for selecting
materials and supervising, developing, and administering IMS activities within the center. This person should also supervise inmate aides
to be assigned to IMS starting in 1975. This should be a half-time
position (although the early days of the program will require more than
half-time effort). As the program becomes developed and as inmate
aides become skilled, the coordinator should be able to delegate considerable amounts of day-to-day work to the aides. Prince George's
County Pay Grade 25, annual salary: $10,000 to $14,000.

Coordinator, job information services, should be available in
1975. This position should be supplied by the state employment service
and need not be a single individual, but should enable the employment
service to assign persons experienced in testing, veterans' affairs,
minority group affairs, employer counseling, and job development.
The position should be a full-time position starting in 1975. Annual
salary, $8,000 to $10,000.

Coordinator, work release, community treatment center, available in 1971. This person should have over-all responsibility for
supervising and managing the work release program and the halfway
house. He should report to the director of the center and be able to
draw on the services and assistance of other staff described in this
section. This person should have experience in working in a community-based treatment center and/or a work release center and be
generally knowledgeable in counseling and guidance, as well as job
development. Prince George's County Pay Grade 25, annual salary,
$10,000 to $14,000.

Work release, community treatment counselors, available on
a part-time basis in 1971. By 1975, there should be the equivalent
of two full-time and one half-time persons employed in this position;
by 1980, the equivalent of three full-time persons. They should have
the over-all function of providing counseling and guidance services
within the work release program and halfway house. They should be
experienced in providing testing and guidance services to inmates and
be able to conduct individual and group counseling programs. Prince
George's County Pay Grade 18, annual salary, $7,000 to $10,000.

Work release, community treatment job development specialist,
available in 1971. This position should start as a half-time position
in 1971, and by 1975, assuming the progress envisioned in this proposal, it should become a full-time position. The responsibilities
of this specialist will be to contact employers who are likely to hire

inmates from the program, provide guidance and counseling to inmates and employers, and generally provide a liaison between the business community and the work release and halfway house programs. The person in this position should be a skilled job development specialist and have some knowledge of the employment situation in the metropolitan community. Prince George's County Pay Grade 18, annual salary, $7,000 to $10,000.

Medical consultant, a medical physician, available on a consultant basis in 1971 to provide health services in the community-based treatment center. By 1975, this person would provide over-all coordination, supervision, and management of the infirmary. This should include physical examinations, diagnoses, prescriptions, and referrals. Also, this person should provide consultant services to the vocational rehabilitation administration regarding the eligibility of inmates for the vocational rehabilitation program, and generally serve as a medical advisor to the social-service center program. The physician should be on-call 20 percent of the time and spend an additional 20 percent of his time in treatment, hospital visits, and so forth. Thus, the cost is about 40 percent of a full-time equivalent annual salary range of $22,000 to $27,000.

Coordinator, vocational rehabilitation program, available on a full-time equivalent basis in 1975. This person should have the major responsibility for selecting, screening, and evaluating applicants for the vocational rehabilitation program, serve as a liaison between the social-service center and the vocational rehabilitation program, and supervise staff persons associated with the vocational rehabilitation program. Annual salary, $10,000 to $12,000.

Vocational rehabilitation counselor, available in 1975 on a full-time equivalent basis. The vocational rehabilitation program should have available one full-time counselor whose major duties will be to provide counseling service to inmates enrolled in the vocational rehabilitation program, evaluation of inmates to determine eligibility and need for vocational rehabilitation services, and follow-up activities within the community. Annual salary range, $7,000 to $10,000.

Vocational rehabilitation specialist, for screening, evaluation, and placement, available on a full-time equivalent basis by 1975. If the program expands, these activities will require the services of at least two full-time professionals. They should have over-all responsibility for screening inmates for eligibility in the vocational rehabilitation program, job development, and rehabilitation services. They should report to the coordinator for vocational rehabilitation. Annual salary, $7,000 to $10,000.

Clerical and secretarial assistants. There should be by 1970, two full-time equivalent clerical-secretarial staff available to the social-service program and community-based treatment facility. By 1980, this should be increased to three full-time persons. Prince George's County Pay Grade 13, annual salary, $5,000 to $8,000.

Inmate aides, available in 1975. There should be five inmate aides employed in the social-service center. These aides should be trained for their positions with the objective that upon release from the detention center, they will be sufficiently trained and experienced to supply full-time employment in the areas in which they have been trained and are working in the detention center. Aides should be employed in the IMS program as library and media aides. At the direction of the IMS coordinator, these aides should be responsible for maintaining day-to-day activities of the library and the simple maintenance, setup, and inspection of media equipment. One full-time aide should be available to the social-service center director to provide assistance in recordkeeping and clerical assistance. In addition, the vocational and job training program and the educational services program should share the services of one full-time inmate aide. Prince George's County Pay Grade 6, salary, $2.00 per hour or $4,000 per year.

ADVISORY COMMITTEE

The sheriff should appoint an advisory committee to the social-service program. The appointment of the committee and its deliberations need not await the construction of the new detention center and the operation of the social-service program. Indeed, the advisory committee should begin to assist the staff to plan for the social-service center and to implement this study. The advisory committee should consist of representatives of agencies that will offer programs in the center, citizens, county officials, inmates, and former inmates.

NOTES

1. "1970 Correctional Officer Salary Survey of Selected Maryland and Virginia and the Washington, D.C. Correctional Systems." (Prepared by the Montgomery County, Maryland Personnel Office, Effective October 1, 1970, 16 pages mimeographed.)

CHAPTER

7

THE
PHYSICAL FACILITY
OF THE
SOCIAL-SERVICE
CENTER

GENERAL REQUIREMENTS, OVER-ALL ATMOSPHERE, AND SETTING

As noted earlier, the social-service center should be a single facility including all social services and should be distinctly different from the institution as a whole. It should be recognized throughout the institution as the focal point for correctional, rehabilitation, learning, and intellectual activities. It should meet three major requirements.

First, the facility should have maximum flexibility in terms of enrollment and participation possibilities. At any one time, the center should be able to accommodate the following kinds of situations: up to 30 individuals should be able to participate in the center as individuals in terms of browsing, selecting materials, using recording equipment, using study carrels, and so forth. The facility should be able to accommodate one-to-one counseling and/or interview situations for up to ten persons at any given time. The facility should accommodate at any one time (up to four) small group sessions involving six to twenty people in any one group.*

Second, the facility should be used by the staff as well as by the inmates. And third, the facility, excluding job training (which

---

*Figure 2, Chapter 4, describes the kinds of participation the social-service program should permit.

should contain about 2,800 square feet) should contain approximately 6,200 square feet. (See Table 27.)

SPACE, STAFF, MATERIALS, AND PROGRAM REQUIREMENTS

As discussed elsewhere, all component programs should be headquartered in the social-service center. Maximum opportunities should be available for inmates to contact various social-service representatives and for these representatives to communicate with each other. Therefore, desk space for the various agencies should be placed throughout the facility.

Table 27 presents a detailed description of requirements for the social-service center program.

TABLE 27

Relationship Between Staff Needs and Space Requirements
for the Social-Service Center

Title	Function	Space Requirements	Equipment	Special Effects
Administrative staff (2 persons)	To coordinate activities related to the social-service center	Office Space: 300 square feet	2 desks and chairs, 3 lounge chairs, coffee-review table, lamp table, bookshelves	Natural light, quiet, refined, not foreboding, comfortable, carpeted, with soft accents
Counseling (2 full-time equivalents)	Establish inmate needs, provide counseling and information to staff charged with social-service responsibilities. May interview individuals or groups	Space for interviews with from 1 to 15 persons to be shared with other functions. (See Conference space.) Groups of larger numbers less rigidly accommodated. Flexibility of prime importance to eliminate duplication of space. Two separate, private offices with 100 square feet, shared with other staff	In each office: desk, 3-drawer file cabinet, desk chair, 2 interview chairs, appropriate shelving	Office and interview areas to be comfortable and easily accessible to inmates. Carpeting and natural light. Counseling-interview areas to be shared with other functions
Secretarial and clerical (2 full-time and 1 part-time)	Usual secretarial and clerical duties	200 square feet for desk work, files, book and reference storage, work space, and small reception area	2 desks with chairs, 4 3-drawer file cabinets, shelving, work table, appropriate seating for reception area	Carpeting and sufficient lighting
Information-media services (IMS)	IMS to serve as a focal point of the center. Multiuse space capable of accommodating individuals alone or in groups of up to 50 persons. Persons may be self- or machine-taught. Movies, filmstrips, slides, opaque projectors, tape recorders, computer terminals, television, etc., to be used here. Earphone headsets to allow overlapping functions. Learning to take place at tables, study carrels, work benches, in lounge chairs, on the floor, or in any position desired. Entirely flexible environment	Square Feet IMS coordinator .... 60 Charge desk .... 60 Card catalog .... 10 Reference table .... 60 Dictionary stand .... 10 Book and periodical shelving .... 720 Reading (50 persons) .... 1,000 Multiuse space .... 1,000 Total 2,920	Coordinator's desk, 3 3-drawer file cabinets, desk with chair, seating and tables for combinations of 1-50 persons, shelving. (See Book and periodical shelving.) 16' chalk board, 16' bulletin board, charge desk, card catalog, reference table, 8 study carrels with space for movie projector, tape recorders, slide projectors, etc. May be modified in future to accommodate computer terminals. Provide sufficient lounge seating, end tables, reference-coffee table, etc, for approximately 8 persons	Space to be thought of as large area divided into smaller areas of varying size by using casual dividers, i.e., book and periodical shelving (counter height). Careful arrangement of lighting, void space, seating, and shelving vital to feeling of separation without enclosure. Space to be purposely oversized to allow many noise-making functions to occur simultaneously. Carpeting, drapes, and paneling mandatory to assure reasonable noise level, while at the same time providing pleasant environment (continued)

TABLE 27 - Continued

Title	Function	Space Requirements	Equipment	Special Effects
Books and periodical shelving	To best serve the population, books and periodicals to be displayed in cell and lounge areas as well as in IMS. Movable shelving on casters necessary; whole sections of books transported and displayed with minimum effort, and IMS to become a flexible facility. (See IMS)	Staff, 500 books, 20 periodicals Inmates, 4,000 books, 10 periodicals Total, 4,500 books, 28 periodicals Linear feet of shelving (lfs) determined as follows: $4{,}500 \text{ books} \times \frac{1 \text{ lfs}}{10 \text{ books}} \times \frac{1 \text{ lfs}}{3 \text{ lf}} = 150 \text{ lfs}$ $90 \text{ periodicals} \times \frac{1 \text{ lfs}}{1 \text{ periodicals}} \times \frac{1 \text{ lfs}}{3 \text{ lf}} = 30 \text{ lfs}$ Total: 180 linear feet of shelving 180 lfs x 4 feet depth = 720 square feet required	150 linear feet of 3-shelf-high, movable, book shelving (mounted on truck wheels); 30 linear feet of 3-shelf-high, movable periodical display case	Depth based on peninsular, divider-type arrangement (See IMS) Note: Care to be taken to assure that a smooth path of travel is provided from the IMS to the cell and lounge areas where books are to be displayed. Use of ramps or elevators may be necessary
Coordinator, information-media services (1 person)	Selects materials, catalogs, shelves, and in general develops a flexible program that will allow maximum dissemination of all materials and use by staff and inmates. Will supervise inmate aides, conduct training programs for inmate aides, and conduct orientation programs and work with inmate committees	60 square feet of floor area within IMS area; no private office space desired	1 desk with chair, and 1 3-drawer file cabinet	Coordinator's desk to be integral part of reading and open stack area, informally placed and easily accessible
Inmate aides (5 persons)	While being trained as library assistants, aides to distribute books, tapes, periodicals, and related educational materials to inmates in cells or lounges	No specific space requirements; aides operate within IMS area	None	None
Equipment storage	Storage of equipment described in Chapter 5	100 square feet	Line walls with 3-foot-deep, adjustable shelving	None
Software storage	House all records, films, tapes, slides, and movies required by IMS programs	100 square feet	Line walls with adjustable shelves 12 inches in depth	None

Title	Function	Space Requirements	Equipment	Special Effects
Conference space	To serve all aspects of the social-service center. Will house groups of from 1 to 16 persons. Flexibility in sound partition arrangement to allow groups of 4-4-4-4, 4-4-8, 8-8, 4-12, or a single group of 16. When conference areas not in use, this area to be used to increase IMS capacity	288 square feet, divisible into modules of 72-72-72-72, 72-72-144, 144-144, 72-216. Groups of larger numbers to be accommodated in a less rigid manner	Conference tables and seating flexible to accommodate groups of 4-4-4-4, 4-4-8, 8-8, 4-12, and 16. Each module equipped with chalkboard	Space to be quiet, refined, and comfortable; light from outside not necessary; carpeting and pleasant surroundings desirable
Employment service	Interviews inmates with regard to careers and job opportunities; may interview 1 person or make presentations to 50	(See Conference space)	(See Conference space)	(See Conference space) Should have access to audiovisual equipment; all areas used by Employment service may be shared with other functions
Vocational rehabilitation staff (2 persons)	Interview inmates, isolate problems, provide assistance as required, set up rehabilitation programs	Provide flexible interview space to accommodate from 1 to 16 persons (See Conference requirements)	(See Conference space)	(See Conference space) Interview space may be shared with other functions
Workspace	Workspace to be used for editing of films, tapes, for development of special projects, for equipment repair, materials development, and for the preparation of displays. Activities may range from 1 person previewing a film to 8 persons making posters	Provide 30 square feet for education personnel and 20 square feet for IMS coordinator, inmate aides, and IMS patrons, all of whom will share this space. 600 square feet total space required	30 linear feet of work counter, 1 work-top sink, 3 3-drawer file cabinets, 2 desks with chairs, 3 counter-high stools, drawers and cabinets for tool and equipment storage, book shelves, 1 corkboard and 1 chalkboard, 4 feet by 8 feet	None
Education (1 full-time and 1 part-time)	Establishes educational programs; interviews and tests to establish needs and levels	Filing space for records and tests; should have separate area for private conferences and testing	1 desk, 1 3-drawer file cabinet; sound room available for review and editing of software	Conference and testing space may be shared with other functions
Maintenance (1 person)	Maintain audiovisual equipment, edit tapes, provide technical background for special presentations, service equipment	Private office not required; provide 50 square feet in work space for desk and workbench, with close proximity to equipment storage	Desk, chair, tool storage, work bench, access to sink	(See Workspace) All new areas may be shared
Production space	Dial access tape system, educational television systems, and recording stage for audiovisual taping; intercom to be connected to lounges, cells, etc.	600 square feet	None	Isolated with respect to sound and light
Recreational consultant	To design and develop recreational programs for inmates, evaluate recreational equipment needs and services	None (share with counseling)	None	None

**ESTIMATED COSTS
TO IMPLEMENT
THE
PROPOSED PROGRAM**

This chapter contains the estimated costs to implement the
program described earlier. Salaries are based on present levels
within Prince George's County, and equipment estimates are based
on current costs. In all cases, one can expect these estimates to
increase 5 percent to 10 percent each year. We have omitted furnish-
ing costs because we assume these items should be part of the expenses for the new facility.

THE PROGRAM PHASES

We recommend that this program be implemented in three
phases beginning in 1971 and ending in 1980. The first phase is designed to improve living conditions in the institution, reduce the
population of the jail, put into a community-based treatment program
into operation, and begin a staff training program. In general, Phase
I is designed as a transition to the planned, new detention center. The
next two phases (Phase II in 1975 and Phase III in 1980) are designed
to implement the entire social-service program.

Phase I, 1971

This phase should be implemented in two steps. The first step
includes staff training, refining procedures, and modernization of
the existing jail. The second step includes the development of a
community-based treatment center (halfway house).

Phase I should include the following elements or components:

1. Community-based treatment facilities for thirty inmates.

2. Extensive counseling, guidance, and job development for inmates assigned to the community-based treatment facility.

3. Counseling, basic education, and limited social services for inmates in the county jail.

4. Remodeling of the existing jail to add air conditioning and an exercise yard.

5. In-service training programs for current staff of the jail.

6. The development of a data-collection system and intake process.

Community-Based Treatment

Up to thirty inmates would be assigned to a community-based treatment facility (halfway house). Also, up to ten former inmates would be assigned on an outpatient basis to the community-treatment facility.

The community-based treatment facility will be a residential facility located near transportation and/or a major population area of the county. Persons assigned to the facility will work or attend school in the community during the day and return to the facility during off-work hours for counseling, guidance, recreation, and so forth. The typical person assigned to the halfway house will spend approximately three months living in the facility and then be assigned on an outpatient basis, whereby he will live in the community and report periodically to the treatment center.

Counseling and Guidance. Persons assigned to the halfway house will have available to them an extensive array of personal and social services and family counseling and guidance, as well as job development, testing, and evaluation services. The staff should provide these services to persons assigned to the facility both as residents and as outpatients on a reservation basis. In addition, the county health department, the state employment service, and other agencies within the community will be called upon to provide special services as required.

In addition, the staff of the community-based treatment facility will also supervise, manage, and conduct extensive counseling and

a basic education program in the county jail. These services will
include designing limited educational and social-service programs
in the jail and providing counseling and guidance to inmates pursuing
these programs. Also, the staff of the community-based treatment
facility will use the services of other social-service agencies within
the community to develop programs.

Air Conditioning and Minor Remodeling of the Existing Jail

The existing jail in Prince George's County is a vastly overcrowded and inadequate facility. During late spring, summer, and
early autumn (about six months of the year), the temperature in the
facility is much too warm to accommodate any reasonable social-
service program. Also, the discomfort in the institution could most
certainly contribute to management problems in the near future.
Second, the institution needs minor remodeling (in terms of the creation of counseling rooms, etc.) to accommodate the program envisioned
above.

Therefore, two major steps should be taken. First, the institution should be air-conditioned to provide some reasonable temperature control. Second, some minor remodeling should be completed in
the institution to accommodate the new program.

Staff Training

There are approximately fifty persons assigned to the existing
county jail on a full-time basis. None of them has received any in-
service or staff training. In part, to prepare the staff for programs
to be conducted in the institution, the sheriff's department should
design and operate training programs for all staff members. The
staff training program should include but not be limited to the following
elements or components: human relations, new methods and concepts
in corrections, dealing with minority groups, correctional administration, and so forth.

Counseling and Limited Social Services in the County Jail

A part-time social-service counselor should be hired in Phase
I to provide services to inmates in the jail. This would be a very
limited program with an undesirably high caseload; but because of
the lack of facilities in the present jail, space is not available. The
counselor will function as a referral agent to existing agencies and
provide limited casework to a total of about fifty individuals per week.

Development of Data Collection and Intake System

The data-intake process in the present jail is inefficient, probably inaccurate, and does not provide information for management or rehabilitation purposes. In Phase I, a feasibility study should be undertaken to evaluate the shortcomings of the present system and design a new system considering the possibility of linking the system to the County's data-processing unit.

Phase II, Approximately 1975

When the new detention center is finished (which we assume will be by 1975), there should be a partial effort to equip and staff the social-service center. In Chapter 7, we indicated how this should be done; the budget that follows lists the cost items.

Phase III, Approximately 1980

By 1980, the social-service center should be fully established.

THE BUDGET

Table 28 lists the annual costs to each agency. These cost estimates are for each phase of the proposed program beginning with a limited program in 1971 for the existing jail and development and implementation of the social-service center programs in the new detention center. Annual operating costs for all programs after full implementation (1981-85) are also provided.

Table 29 presents the detailed cost estimates for implementing each phase of the proposed program. For each phase, the estimated cost of each item is presented. A code letter is given for the agency or department providing funding and/or administrative responsibility. In reading the table, the following should be kept in mind:

Under personnel, items 1-4, 25, and portions of 24 represent a transfer of resources within the Sheriff's Department. By 1980, items 1-4, 12, 13, and 25 will represent a transfer of resources within the sheriff's department. Items 5-23 represent staff supported by federal funds and/or other agencies. In most cases, the staff will be provided by federal funds initially and ultimately supported on a full-time basis by county and state agencies. These agencies

TABLE 28

Estimated Annual Costs to Each Agency

Agency or Department	Agency Codes[a]	1971	1975	1980	1981-85
Prince George's County					
Sheriff's Department	A	$ 74,800[b]	126,300[c]	$236,800[d]	$358,800[e]
Board of Education	B	2,000	22,000	35,000	31,000
Library	C	9,000	21,000	23,000	17,000
Health Department	D	10,000	18,000	16,000	10,000
Maryland State					
Employment Service	E	8,000	18,500	18,500	18,500
Division of Vocational Rehabilitation	F	00	58,500	78,500	78,500
Department of Education	G	00	53,000	27,000	12,000
Other county agencies	H	15,000	15,000	15,000	15,000
Law Enforcement Assistance Administration, U.S. Department of Justice	I	270,000	204,500	129,000	00
Total		$388,800	$536,800	$578,800	$540,800

Note: Costs for each agency do not necessarily represent new cash outlay. Some services will represent a transfer to existing resources. We have indicated the amount of new money vs. transfer of resources in the Sheriff's Department but did not have access to financial information for the other agencies.

Following is an example of transfer of resources: If a community-based treatment center or halfway house is developed, this will result in reducing the jail population by about 30 persons. This will result in less custodial care, lodging, food, and other expenses in the existing jail. These reduced expenses can be transferred to the new activities. New money refers to additional expenses above existing outlays. It should be understood that both terms represent approximations subject to variations of 10 percent to 15 percent due to inflation, salary adjustments, new technology, and so forth.

[a]Letters correspond to agency codes in Table 29.
[b]About $30,000 will be transfer of resources and about $45,000 will be new money.
[c]About $35,000 will be transfer of resources and about $92,000 will be new money.
[d]About $32,000 will be transfer of resources and about $205,000 will be new money.
[e]About $210,000 will be transfer of resources and about $150,000 will be new money.

TABLE 29

Estimated Costs to Implement the Proposed Program

	Phase I, 1971		Phase II, 1975		Phase III, 1980		Annual Operating Costs, 1981-85	
Cost Item (1)	Total Cost (2)	Agency Code[a] (3)	Annual Cost (4)	Agency Code[a] (5)	Annual Cost (6)	Agency Code[a] (7)	Annual Cost (8)	Agency Code[a] (9)
I. Personnel[b]								
1. County sheriff	$ 3,600	A $	$ 2,400	A $	$ 2,400	A $	$ 2,400	A
2. Deputy sheriffs	7,200	A	5,000	A	5,000	A	5,000	A
3. Warden	3,600	A	2,400	A	2,400	A	2,400	A
4. Custodial staff	14,600	A	5,000	A	5,000	A	5,000	A
5. Director, social-service center	15,000	I	15,000	A	15,000	A	15,000	A
6. Assistant director, social-service center	00		12,500	I	12,500	A	12,500	A
7. Coordinator, educational services	00		6,000	I		B 6,000 / I 6,000	12,000	B
8. Social-service counselors	4,500	I	18,000	A 4,500 / I 13,500	18,000	A	18,000	A
9. Coordinator, job and	00		6,000	I	12,000	B 6,000 / I 6,000	12,000	B
10. vocational training								
10. Coordinator, IMS	4,000	C	6,000	C	12,000	C	12,000	C
11. Coordinator, job information services	00		9,000	E	9,000	E	9,000	E
12. Coordinator work-release and community-treatment programs	14,000	I	14,000	A	14,000	A	14,000	A
13. Work-release, community-treatment counselors	24,000	I	30,000	A-24,000 / I- 6,000	36,000	A30,000 / I 6,000	36,000	A
14. Work-release, community-treatment job development specialist	4,500	E	9,000	E	9,000	E	9,000	E
15. Medical consultant	10,000	D	10,000	D	10,000	D	10,000	D
16. Medical corpsmen	00		12,000	A	12,000	A	12,000	A
17. Vocational rehabilitation medical and psychological counselors	00		10,000	F	10,000	F	10,000	F
18. Coordinator, vocational rehabilitation program	00		11,000	F	11,000	F	11,000	F
19. Vocational rehabilitation counselor	00		9,000	F	9,000	F	9,000	F
20. Vocational rehabilitation specialist	00		8,500	F	8,500	F	8,500	F
21. Vocational rehabilitation instructors	00		20,000	F	40,000	F	40,000	F
22. Education, training and data processing consultants	30,000	I	10,000	A	10,000	A	10,000	A
23. Education and staff-training instructors	4,000	I	2,000	I	2,000	G	2,000	G
24. Secretarial and clerical Staff	11,500	A 1,500 / I 10,000	12,000	A 10,000 / I 2,000	18,000	A 12,000 / A 6,000	18,000	A
25. Inmate aides	00		20,000	A	20,000	A	20,000	A

Cost Item (1)	Phase I, 1971 Total Cost (2)	Agency Code[a] (3)	Phase II, 1975 Annual Cost (4)	Agency Code[a] (5)	Phase III, 1980 Annual Cost (6)	Agency Code[a] (7)	Annual Operating Costs, 1981-85 Annual Cost (8)	Agency Code[a] (9)
II. Travel and expenses	4,500	I	5,000	I	5,000	I	5,000	A
III. Materials and services								
1. Educational services	7,000	A 2,000 B 2,000 I 3,000	20,000	B	21,000	B	5,000	B
2. Recreational services	2,000	A	2,000	B	2,000	B	2,000	B
3. Information media services	5,000	C	15,000	C	11,000	C	5,000	C
4. Job information services	1,500	E	500	E	500	E	500	E
5. Work and education release	300	A	500	I	500	A	500	A
6. Job training	00		53,000	G	25,000	G	10,000	G
7. Community-based treatment	150,000	I	150,000	I	175,000	I 100,000 A 75,000	175,000	A
8. Health services	2,000	E	8,000	D	6,000	D	5,000	A
9. Staff training	2,000	I	1,000	I	1,000	A	1,000	A
10. Miscellaneous	2,000	I	2,000	A	2,000	A	2,000	A
IV. Remodeling	47,000	A 40,000 I 7,000	00		-0-		00	
V. Professional services	15,000	H	15,000	H	15,000	H	15,000	H
Total Cost	$388,800		$536,800		$578,800		$540,800	

[a]This column presents a code for agencies with program responsibility and/or agencies providing funds for each cost item. Codes refer to agencies as follows:

A - Prince George's County Sheriff's Department
B - Prince George's County Board of Education
C - Prince George's County Library
D - Prince George's County Health Department
E - Maryland State Employment Service

F - Maryland Division of Vocational Rehabilitation
G - Maryland State Department of Education
H - Other Prince George's County Agencies
I - Law Enforcement Assistance Administration, United States Department of Justice

[b]Personnel salaries assume a midpoint in the salary ranges presented in Chapter 6. Annual increases should be expected at approximately 10 percent or following county pay scales. Generally, all salaries and increases should follow county or state pay scales. Fringe benefits are not included in the estimates but should be included at least 25 percent of the personnel costs allocated to each agency or department.

may decide to reassign existing staff and resources to the program
or provide new money. Specific descriptions of each staff position
are included in Chapter 6.

Under travel and expenses, minimal travel costs to be incurred
by staff in the program are included.

Items listed under materials and services include costs for each
of the programs of the social-service center. Explanation of specific
materials necessary for most of these programs is included in Chapter
5. In most cases, agencies will provide the materials and services
initially. The community-based treatment center will be supported
with federal funds until 1980 when it will be partially supported by the
sheriff's department, and in 1981, totally supported by the sheriff's
department. This program will represent a transfer of resources
and will not require new money. If the program progresses as proposed here, the sheriff's department may assume these costs earlier.

Items listed under remodeling will initially include remodeling
of the present jail and remodeling and/or renovations required in
the community-based treatment center.

Professional services should include services to be provided by
other county agencies to implement and maintain the programs. These
services include legal, fiscal and accounting, data processing, and so
forth. This support may increase as the program becomes fully
implemented.

9

**FINDINGS
AND
RECOMMENDATIONS**

MAJOR FINDINGS

Part III presents the major findings and conclusions as succinctly as possible. In many cases, we use simple and stark terms, and probably over- and/or understate the basic ideas. Thus, the reader should not only review these findings but the basis for the findings which are in other chapters of this volume. Nevertheless, our basic findings follow.

1. More than 7,000 persons are processed annually through Prince George's County Jail.

2. The number of persons processed through the county detention system will grow steadily through 1980 at which time it could total 9,000 to 13,000. We estimate that the jail is now serving 20 to 30 persons per day, but will, by 1980, be serving 30 to 40 persons daily, or an increase of about 30 percent.

3. The overwhelming majority of persons passing through the jail are poor, underemployed or unemployed, and have social, personal, and other problems.

4. The majority of persons processed through the jail are charged with relatively minor offenses.

5. Except for emergency physical care, inmates processed through the jail do not receive social services.

6. The majority processed through the jail stay for relatively short periods of time (about 50 percent stay for less than 24 hours).

7. Because of the large number of persons who move through the jail each year, this institution is an ideal social-service delivery point for the county.

8. The jail at any one time contains a large number of people who have been in the institution for several months and could, if programs were available, be enrolled in a variety of social-service programs.

9. The present facility is vastly overcrowded and almost completely lacks facilities for social-service programs; thus, it would not be practical (perhaps not even possible) to develop any extensive, meaningful, social-service programs in the present facility.

10. Many persons processed through the jail need social services and could benefit from an imaginative and integrated social-service program.

11. State and county agencies have almost completely ignored the need for the provision of services in Prince George's County Jail.

RECOMMENDATIONS

Our general recommendation is that an extended program of social services be included in the planned detention center. This program should become the hub of the social-service and rehabilitation program within the new institution. Our most important recommendations are listed below:

1. The program can be implemented in three phases, the first of which can be developed before the new detention center is constructed   Phase I consists of two steps: The first provides staff training and improvement of living conditions in the existing jail. The second step is the development of a community-based treatment center (halfway house). Phases II and III are concerned with the development of the social-service program and facility in the new detention center.

2. The social-service facility should be designed as an imaginative combination of programs within the institution. It should contain approximately 6,200 square feet. The facility should be clearly identified as different from the over-all institution in terms of decor, climate, staff, attitudes, and so forth. It should be a place that inmates and staff alike view as the central location within the institution for social, rehabilitative, and educational services.

3. Activities within the center should be under the direction of an experienced administrator, the social-service center director, who should be responsible for coordinating all services within the center.

4. Local agencies within the county and state should offer programs within the social-service center. Services should include education, training, counseling, vocational rehabilitation, library services, recreation, and so forth.

5. Each person passing through the institution should be made aware of the social-service center. When an individual leaves the institution, the services should again be called to his attention. In the event that the person desires assistance, these services should either be provided him while he is in the institution or he should be referred to agencies on the outside.

6. Every inmate who stays more than five days in the institution should, on a voluntary basis, be tested, counseled, and interviewed for eligibility for a planned program of social services.

7. Once an inmate is considered eligible for social services, the center staff or the vocational rehabilitation program should be responsible for designing a prescription of services for the individual; the services will be provided either by the center or by the division of vocational rehabilitation.

8. The social-service center should provide for instruction and counseling programs at a variety of levels, including services within the center for individuals or small groups or services via electronic transmission from the center to individuals confined to their cells.

9. The social-service center should have an advisory committee composed of custodial staff, county officials, representatives from social-service agencies, inmates, and former inmates.

10. The program can be implemented in three phases starting in 1971 and ending in 1980. The total cost of Phase I (1971) will be about $390,000, of which about $270,000 will come from the federal government, about $45,000 from state and county agencies, and $75,000 from the sheriff's department. This phase will result in a halfway house, modernization of the jail, staff training, and an improved inmate data-collection system.

During Phase II (1975 or when the new detention center is completed), the social-service center will begin to function and will cost $540,000, of which federal agencies will provide about $205,000, state and local agencies will also provide $205,000, and the sheriff's department will provide $125,000.

Phase III (1980) will represent complete implementation of the program at a cost of about $580,000, of which Federal agencies can provide $130,000, state and local agencies about $110,000, and the sheriff's department about $240,000.

11. Actual cost of the program in new money will be considerably less than the above point suggests. An important feature of the plan is that a large share of the program can be funded by transfer of resources in the sheriff's department (facilities, staff, etc.) from existing programs (largely part of the cost of the operation of the jail) to the proposed program. For example, operation of the program (after 1980) will cost about $540,000 of which 40 percent ($210,000) can come from a transfer of resources presently being spent in the sheriff's department; county and state agencies can provide about $190,000. Thus, a total of about $150,000 annually in new money will be required from the sheriff's department.

**APPENDIX:
PRESENT
AND PROPOSED
INMATE
FLOW**

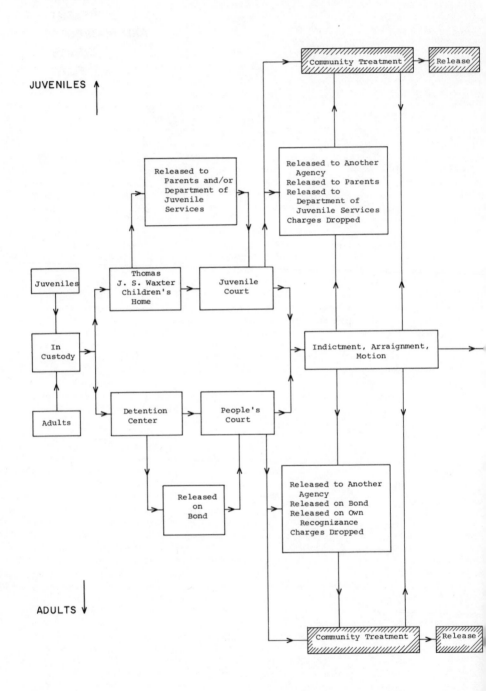

JUVENILES ↑

Released to
Parents and/or
Department of
Juvenile
Services

Released to Another
  Agency
Released to Parents
Released to
  Department of
  Juvenile Services
Charges Dropped

Community Treatment

Release

Thomas
J. S. Waxter
Children's
Home

Juvenile
Court

Juveniles

In
Custody

Adults

Indictment, Arraignment,
Motion

Detention
Center

People's
Court

Released
on
Bond

Released to Another
  Agency
Released on Bond
Released on Own
  Recognizance
Charges Dropped

ADULTS ↓

Community Treatment

Release

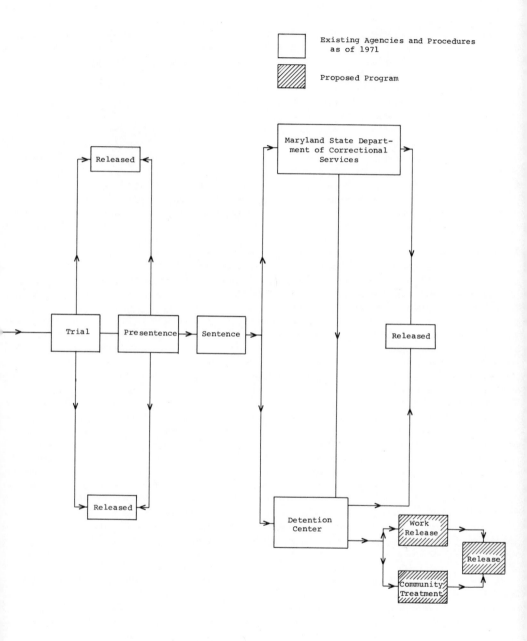

Existing Agencies and Procedures as of 1971

Proposed Program

ABOUT THE AUTHOR

Social, Educational Research and Development, Inc. (SERD) is a social-science, educational research, and human development corporation specializing in social and educational research, training, development, and consulting services. The firm was founded in 1964 and serves private industry, public and private agencies, schools and colleges, libraries, hospitals, prisons, and community groups in the areas of education, training, social, psychological, and economic research, minority-group relations, and community development.

SERD has completed a number of projects in the correctional field including prison studies, interviews of former convicts, educational problems of prisoners, and is presently operating a halfway house for former offenders in Washington, D.C.

The firm has home offices in Silver Spring, Maryland—a suburb of Washington, D.C.—and branch offices in Chicago, Honolulu, Washington, D.C., and the U.S. Virgin Islands.